To: Elaine

Glenside Kid

Best Regards,

Ted Taylor

The Glenside Kid

The Glenside Kid
© Ted Taylor, 2011

All Rights Reserved
Printed in the United States of America

This is a work of mostly creative non-fiction. Just about all the events described in this book really happened – at least this is the way I remember them or wanted them to be. Some of the names have been changed to avoid potential lawsuits, but many others haven't. A few characters are blends of several real people to make them more interesting. If someone is offended I'm sorry, if they feel left them out that's probably because I did. The fact that you are offended or excluded was either accidental, subliminal, coincidental or maybe just that I didn't remember you. The other possibility is that it is the fault of my over-active imagination.

To order additional copies of this book contact:
TTA LLC, P. O. Box 273, Abington PA 19001 or the publisher.
1-877-576-7212

Published by
The Educational Publisher
www.EduPublisher.com
1313 Chesapeake Ave.
Columbus, OH 43212

Autobiography, nostalgia
Taylor, Henry R. (Ted) 1940-
The Taylor & Roth families
Glenside, PA (Cheltenham & Abington Townships)
Carmel Presbyterian Church
Philadelphia Athletics/Connie Mack
Philadelphia Eagles football club
Willow Grove Park

ISBN: 1-934849-56-1
ISBN 13: 978-1-934849-56-9

Cover art by Cynthia M. Taylor
Photos, Roth Family Archives, Taylor Family Archives,
Public Domain or other stuff I came across in boxes in the attic

Other books by Ted Taylor –

Baseball Cards – 300 All-Time Stars
The Official Baseball Card Collecting Handbook

100 Year & 100 Recipes
(The Story of Ralph's Italian Restaurant)

The Philadelphia Athletics Trilogy

The Philadelphia Athletics by the Numbers
The Ultimate Philadelphia Athletics Reference Book, 1901-1954
The Duke of Milwaukee, the Life & Times of Al Simmons

Textbooks

Introduction to Mass Communications
Introduction to Public Relations

Checklist Book

Phillies Baseball Card & Memorabilia Checklist Book (1979)

*This Book is dedicated to my wife Cindy,
My Mom & Two Dads...
Jean Shepherd who inspired me...
And all my pals from Glenside PA*

Contents

Prologue	ix
"The Glenside Kid" Poem	xx
I – We're going to meet the twins	1
II – First there was Jack, then Helen, then me	3
III – By the sea	12
IV – The kid gets cooked, as does Dad's goose	14
V – What is it about celebrities?	20
VI – We meet the Sons of the Pioneers	23
VII – We drive the Benz to the hospital	28
VIII – The 1940 Plymouth	29
IX – Bored to death in the waiting room	34
X – An Eagles game with Uncle Charlie	37
XI – The twins almost lived in Glenside too	43
XII – Glenside was the Kid's "Hometown"	46
XIII – Negotiate but don't back down	55
XIV – Billy Buck and I do battle	56
XV – All the nuts are not in the jar	63
XVI – Glenside had its share of characters	64
XVII – Getting a glove and cap for Brett II	69
XVIII – Connie Mack and me	71
XIX – Ten months until Christmas	78
XX – The Glenside Kid saves Christmas	79
XXI – We've always been joiners	82
XXII – The Glenside Kid joins a gang	85
XXIII – The weatherman cuts us a break	90
XXIV – Let it $now	91
XXV – The first day of the rest of their lives	96
XXVI – Nyoka, Queen of the Jungle	98
XXVII – Setting up a legacy	102
XXVIII – The baseball card Kid	103
XXIX – Helping their friend the dentist	109
XXX – A fate worse than death	110
XXXI – Not much of a skater	114
XXXII – Red Rascal Roller Skates	115
XXXIII – Wonder how the cats will like the twins	117
XXXIV – My best pet was half-a-dog	119
XXXV – The Taylor kids were not caught up in sports	124
XXXVI – The kid gets a dose of reality	126
XXXVII – Doing stuff with the kids	136

XXXVIII – Gone fishing with Ernie	137
XXXVIX – Junior High days	141
XL – I help close the park	146
XLI – Life was a lark, so said the ad	148
XLII – Not Irish Twins	151
XLIII – Waking up my sister	152
XLIV – Religion is still important today	155
XLV – Christ was my Sunday School teacher	157
XLVI – The things we did for a buck	163
XLVII – Facebook, who needs it?	171
XLVIII – Chuck, Charlie, Cholly & Charles	172
XLIX – Time Marches On	177
L – The past is prologue	178

Book 2

"The Glenside Kid Rides Again"	189
Chapter One – Rocking my world	191
Chapter Two – The Kid does battle with Cancer	193
Chapter Three – Don't worry it'll feel just like a pin prick	196
Chapter Four – We tell Dr. Lyons what the plan will be	200
Chapter Five – I begin Radiation treatments	203
Chapter Six – We enter the final phase	205
Epilogue	211
About the Author	213
Index	215

I know very dimly when I start to write what's going to happen. I just have a very general idea, and then the thing develops as I write.

— Aldous Huxley

The Glenside Kid

The Glenside Kid

Prologue...

My very first memory, ever, of anything is of being a little kid standing on the basement steps of our brown stucco twin house on the middle of the block in Glenside and hearing that President Franklin D. Roosevelt had just died. I was four. The announcer was Arthur Godfrey. Do the math it's 1945, this makes me old. But it's like a snapshot burned in to my memory. I can conjure it up anytime I want. I see it crystal clear. Just like it was yesterday.

I was in what Mom called the cellar way, blue-grey wooden steps, white concrete wall, a shelf with soft drinks on it. At the foot of the stairs was a large converted coal furnace transformed some time ago in to an oil burner, Mom's sparkling white wringer washer was opposite that. Asbestos wrapped heat pipes running the length of the cellar, an oil tank at the other end of the basement, an empty coal bin, and a trap door that took you under the front porch where, for some reason, reposed a stash of old glass milk bottles. Priceless collectibles today. Dad's workbench, with a vice attached to it that was large enough to suspend a '35 Chevy, along with tools that neither of us ever used very much, lined the other wall. There was a Ping Pong table that served provided recreation and alternately as my train platform every Christmas.

As a boy growing up in the Philadelphia suburbs right after World War II I feel that I lived in a much safer world than we do now. Sure, as a little kid I was scared silly of the Japs and frightened of Hitler, but I knew that I was safe because the Soldiers, Sailors and Marines – some of them family members - would protect me. I loved being a kid in Glenside and cherished every moment of it. I cannot imagine a better place or a better era to grow up in.

There were two baseball teams in town – the Phillies and the Athletics (the A's) – and, to a little boy like me, baseball was the most important sport of all. Football and basketball were the activities that filled in the gaps between baseball seasons. As I got a little older my Mom thought it was okay if my pals and I walked to

The Glenside Kid

the Reading Railroad station in Glenside and took the train to North Philly and walked from there to the baseball game. Since we had a team in each league, there was always a game there on weekends between April and the end of September.

Of course taking that train was a big deal. My pals and I were probably 12 or 13 years old when we first did it, we'd walk to the Glenside train station, buy our ticket from the man in the cage windowed booth, go out on the platform and wait for the train. Once aboard – and the conductor punched our tickets - we'd sail through Jenkintown, Elkins Park, Fern Rock, Wayne Junction and the rest of the stations until we arrived at the North Broad Street Station – a majestic, white columned building located across the street from what-was-once the Phillies ballpark (Baker Bowl). Quickly piling off the train we'd saunter down Lehigh Avenue to 21st Street and enter the promised land of Shibe Park. It was a mythic place and, to this day, no other ball park I've ever been in (and I've been in lots of them, coast-to-coast) compares with it. In my den are two green-painted seats from that old ball yard – seats that were originally installed there in 1909.

My Dad, Jack, died in June, 1949, when I was eight. We were probably poor, though Mom (Helen) never let on. But I do know that the main reason I dislike steak to this day is because my Mother would serve something for Sunday dinner and call it "steak". What it was, I later realized, was liver. So as a consequence I dislike steak and hate liver. When other kids in the neighborhood would rave about their mother's serving steak for dinner I thought they were all crazy. Staples at our dinner table included chicken dishes, hot dogs, Spam and fried/breaded egg plant. I also loved meat loaf and the Chun King chicken chow mein that Mom would extract from a can. I loved spaghetti and the wonderful sauce that came out of that *San Giorgio* can. We made do; I thought we were doing fine. Life was good, I was happy. I still like to eat that stuff today.

After Dad died Mom provided such a good home environment for me that I never really thought much about what I was missing until she remarried Ernie Lay in 1956. He assumed the Father role that all kids need and he did it so seamlessly that it all went unnoticed by me then. He was certainly a special man, but what did I know? I was growing up and having a great time. My father, Jack, was always "Dad". My step father, Ernie, was always "Pop".

The town of Glenside had been home to my Mom's family, the Roth's, since 1874 or so and I fit right in. The family seemed to know everyone. The church, in our case Carmel Presbyterian, was the hub of our social and spiritual existence. Mom was the assistant superintendent of the Cradle Roll department and I earned countless perfect attendance medals for never missing out on Sunday School. When your mother is a Sunday School big shot you don't miss many classes.

I probably wasn't the keenest observer of things – though as I write this book I realize that I haven't forgotten much either - and it didn't dawn on me at the time that we weren't exactly rolling in money. One of my Mom's best friends, Mildred, was the wife of a budding millionaire contractor. This friendship provided lots of good things, including summer day trips to wherever they were vacationing – but all I really needed to know about her was that she had a large TV and we used to walk over there and watch Milton Berle ("We're the men of Texaco, we work from Maine to Mexico", they'd sing at the start) on Tuesday nights. Her husband, Thomas, is gone, so is she, but his company remains one of the most prosperous contracting businesses in the area and you still see his trucks all over the place.

My Mom's friend also had a daughter. She was a year older than me. I know that they would have loved it if Mary Ann and I had found some chemistry. We didn't. At least none more than brother and sister – yet we remained friends until college when, just as I arrived as a freshman at Millersville STC, she transferred to another school and we never really connected again. Later in life she assumed the company's direction and, I hear, only recently retired.

The Glenside Kid

I loved my elementary school in Glenside. At least most of the time. It was, to me, a majestic, magical, old building with a ramp running up the side of the building to the auditorium. For some reason we called this ramp "The Castle" and it figured prominently in our fantasy games. I thought that the teachers were the most wonderful people who ever lived. Several of them helped influence me along a career path – which I have spent mostly in education.

The school was on Spring House Lane at the lower end of my street, no more than a half-a-block away. If school started at 8.30, I could leave the house at 8.25 and still have time to spare – it was downhill to school, uphill on the way home.

Glenside School, 1950. I'm nine and in fourth grade. That's me second from left, second row. In this class is a future country & western songwriter, a future long term member of the Georgia State legislature, several successful business owners, a couple of teachers and, of course, an author. I can name every one of them.

I remember the day we met Mrs. Shepherd (my fourth grade teacher, first name Florence) in downtown Glenside at the Acme supermarket. I was amazed. I didn't know that teachers had a life outside of school. Clearly she ate like us mere mortals. Imagine that. I guess I didn't think much about stuff like that in those days. Even though the A&P was right across the street, we were Acme people and only went to the other market as a last resort.

The Glenside Kid

My first crush was in kindergarten. The object of my affection? Miss Dorothy Sudlow, the very blonde, very pretty, teacher. Nothing came of it. The age difference and all, I suppose. I also learned about death very young when our homeroom teacher, Miss Jane McAfee, died mid-way through fourth grade, I believe she was in her mid-20's Anyway she was much too young. All the kids took it hard; I already knew about death and realized that it was just a part of life. Still, if I dwelled on it, it would scare the daylights out of me. And sometimes I did. To be honest, just the idea that someday there could be nothing still unnerves me. It's why I believe in God.

Thomas Williams Junior High in Wyncote was a lot of fun and a great time in my life. For the first time I took the bus to school. That was cool. Because I played sports, though, I usually walked home. I also found out that I liked girls and was always in love with somebody. I thought they were pretty neat. I had always hung out with girls, but that was different. My neighbor Carolyn was a helluva baseball player and she went to Phillies and A's baseball and Temple University football games with me, but she was a pal, a fellow sports nut, but never my girl friend. But Sherry Woodstock was my first real heart-thumping girlfriend. She was little and cute, lived a block away, was in my homeroom and we went to dance class at Curtis Hall together. The dance class did me little good, I had then and have to this day two left feet, but I liked being with her.

Then there was Norma Silver who lived nearby (what a curvy creature she was), and Claire Maxwell and Bonnie Straus and Dottie McKay. And this was just junior high. School newspaper advisor, Mrs. Nellie Neide hooked me on journalism in 8th grade and I became a writer, ultimately the editor, for *The Mascot,* the official school newspaper. When I achieved 40-column inches of published material I got a "Mascot" pin for my lapel. It told the world I was a published writer.

Across the street from my house lived Walter "Dipper" Wilson, an editor with *The Philadelphia Bulletin* and he told me about the wonders of working for a newspaper. It seemed like a potential career for me. (Years later I almost took a job with Dipper's paper, but didn't. Good thing, too. It folded shortly after that. Dipper would have been proud, years later, when I wrote a weekly column for 12 years in *The Philadelphia Daily News.*)

Cheltenham High School was another revelation. I got my first car, a 1950 Ford; I played a little football, a little baseball, ran some cross country, played around in my studies, sang in the chorus, served on student council and had my first serious love affair. She was Ginny Hudson with the light brown hair. She was a sophomore and pretty as a picture, I was a senior. She looked like Shirley MacLaine, was Catholic, I was Presbyterian. In those days that was going to spell trouble – and it did.

Her Mother disliked me with a passion – to her I was the Anti-Christ. She seemed to know what I was up to. (Was I that obvious?) In her Mother's eyes I was just a step above pond scum. I figured it was because I was a Protestant; maybe she just didn't like me. I think her dad thought I was okay. Eventually her Mother, who made Margaret Hamilton's Wicked Witch seem sweet by comparison, managed to break us up. It's a long story, how she did it. But I hated her for it and I don't, as a rule, really ever hate anybody. Dislike them a lot, sure. But, hate? Nope. But in her case I made an exception.

Ginny eventually married a classmate of mine. A big red-headed Presbyterian guy named Harry. I married a beautiful Italian Catholic girl named Cindy. We both made good choices and have had long marriages – and continue to be friends. Cindy still refers to her as "your old girl friend" – a little jealousy from your wife after 40-plus years of marriage is good for the ego. That Ginny and I both found compatible mates was neat. It's how things work sometimes. Her Mom? Long dead. I didn't make it to the funeral.

Sports have always been a huge part of my life. It seems that every school I attended, almost every line of work I go in to, I end up in sports. In junior high I just played football – and wasn't that bad as I recall – though I did drop a pass once in the end zone against our arch rival – Glenside Weldon - and we had to settle for a 6-6 tie. At Cheltenham high school I played football as a 135 pound defensive back and the only game my mom ever saw me play (as a junior) they carried me off the field when I failed to stop a 6'2, 235-lb. runaway freight train named Rollie West.

As I recall I played on just one unbeaten team in my entire athletic career – and that includes a lot of teams. It was the 1957 YMCA league basketball champion Carmel Presbyterian Church club that went 14-and-0. I wish I could say I was a star, but I was, at best, "the sixth man". Still winning every game was a real hoot. (In the interest of full disclosure my friend Chuck says that our junior high football team went unbeaten in my last year there, I don't remember that.)

In college I played baseball (not all that well, but I made the team as a freshman and that was a good thing) and whenever I was home, since I was a little kid on the Glenside Midgets, I played sandlot ball – I even was on a team in Glenside with a youngster named Reggie Jackson. As fate would have it, Jackson was "the little kid" – younger by four years than the rest of us - on the team and I was the star pitcher. When I wasn't playing hardball I was playing for my church softball team. At Millersville State Teachers College I missed almost two weeks of the first season when I came down with the measles. Best game for me was against Lincoln University. I got four hits. Lincoln is a black college, one of the nation's oldest, but this day their pitcher was a white kid and he was awful. It was like batting practice.

I signed on at Drexel University right out of college and, presto, I was the sports information director. Drexel was where I met my wife. She was one of the office secretary's. I often tell people that she worked for me for two years – and I've been working for her ever since.

The boss was named John Tully and he steered me along a path in public relations that provided the basis for my livelihood for

The Glenside Kid

decades. John urged me to get my professional public relations certification (APR) in the early 1970's. Despite my full-time jobs, and because we thought it more important that Cindy stay home and raise our four kids, I needed a second job and became a sportscaster on a Philadelphia radio station doing high school football and basketball games for well over a dozen years. I also became a disc jockey and talk show host. On the side I officiated high school football and coached both midget football and baseball. At Drexel I got to be with the legendary basketball coach Sam Cozen and to preside over their last couple of seasons as a college football team.

Leaving Drexel for the post of Public Relations Director (and teacher of freshman English) at Ursinus College it was just a year before Dr. Donald L. Helferich signed me up as the coach of the varsity baseball team. My first club won five more games than my predecessor and led the league in hitting – I could always teach hitting. And so it went. I looked so young that everyone thought I was a player and, once, I almost did play when half of our team got lost on the way to Western Maryland University for a game. Lucky for us all, a car load of my players got there before I was about to take the field as one of them.

PMC Colleges then hired me to change the name of the institution to Widener College (now University). I was PR director and, thanks to Fitz Eugene Dixon's money, got to handle all the marketing things they wanted to do and, mostly, got to do the publicity for Billy "White Shoes" Johnson (now an NFL Hall of Famer) and was on campus when the Eagles held their pre-season camps there. Billy was something. He scored 60 touchdowns for the Pioneers in three seasons. He was the best football player I ever saw – at any level. Best thing about Widener was that Cindy and I got to spend considerable time at Oxford University in England one summer (1973) as part of a program sponsored by the college.

My next stop was Spring Garden College, I went in as VP for external affairs and just a couple of years later, and with a new president on board, I became director of athletics. The new guy, Dan DeLucca, said, "I can always get someone to handle the fund

The Glenside Kid

raising, alumni and PR, but there aren't many around like you who know so much about athletics". I took the job, it lasted 14 years. Sports, always sports.

From there it was on to professional golf where I got to run the PGA's Philadelphia Section for three years – and became a reasonably average player, I liked the game and once shot a 70. But golf pros can be prima donnas and the Philly section had more than its share (some where real pains). Being executive director meant being buddy buddy with whoever was in power at the time. It got old very quickly.

And then education called my name again and in 1989 I went back to the college scene, where I became Athletic Director at Philadelphia College of Textiles & Science (now, Philadelphia University). As boss of the Rams athletics department I got to work with Basketball Hall of Famer Herb Magee who had also been acting AD before I arrived in East Falls. I'll never forget the day I arrived. Herb was walking out the door, took one look at me, said "Thank God you are here" and tossed me the keys to the building. We were actually both glad I was there.

After three-plus very nice years at Textile, the private sector beckoned and I became VP of hobby sales and marketing for the Fleer Corporation (producers of sports trading cards and that American tradition Double Bubble bubble gum). Paul Mullan who had, a decade earlier, tried to hire me to run the baseball card operation at Donruss, made me one of those offers I couldn't refuse. Yet, had I known he'd sell the company two years later (to Marvel Entertainment) I'd have never left the college. With Fleer I travelled all over the US, became a regular at the Super Bowl, NBA All-Star game, Baseball All-Star game and hung out with some of the best players in sports.

When I left Fleer I joined a company called The Scoreboard in Cherry Hill, NJ. It was a disaster. Six months later I left – just went home one day and never came back - and formed my own PR company where sports accounts immediately became a priority. I

The Glenside Kid

had the connections, knew the people. And I was tired of working for others. The business blossomed and I handled some very interesting and widely varied accounts outside of sports – including Ralph's in South Philly, the oldest family-owner Italian restaurant in America, Act II Playhouse, a professional equity theatre, in Ambler, several of the Lee's Hoagie House restaurants and the Tel Hai Retirement Community in Chester County.

I've guest hosted a nationally syndicated sports radio show "Ron Barr's Sports By-Line USA" well over 50 times (a couple of times from their home studio in San Francisco), made a couple of national appearances as a host on "Fox in the Zone" (once in Dallas, TX where I hosted an on-camera tour of a large baseball card printing facility), have done countless local radio and TV shows and, for good measure, have written five books about baseball – not counting this one, the two textbooks, the checklist book or the Ralph's cookbook.

And now as a sports authenticator and appraiser I have parlayed my 45 years of hobby experience – as a collector of baseball cards and sports memorabilia - in to a business that works with auction houses, collectors, dealers and insurance companies. Along the way I have built a pretty good collection of sports treasures of my own. People ask me why I don't try to expand the business and I explain, "I'm as busy as I want to be". A nice thing.

In "real life" I am also still involved in education and, since 2000, have been an adjunct professor of business communications at Chestnut Hill College – at the other end of Germantown Avenue from where I spent 14 years doing many different things at Spring Garden College. I've taught public relations, mass communications, journalism, creative writing, introduction to literature and public speaking during my tenure "on the hill".

My task of earning a living has been an adventure. I have had lots of jobs, most of them fun – there were also some stinkers, but they're best forgotten. My best friend Jack Andrews (two days younger than me, as he always points out) once paid me the ultimate compliment, "Ted knows how to make a buck", he said. I've tried.

There is, however, something about my life that kind of eats at me. See if you can detect a pattern here. I lived on Oak Road, we had the only oak tree – it got hit by lightening a couple of years ago and is gone. I went to Glenside Elementary School, they closed and later demolished the building. I went to Thomas Williams Junior High – it is now a parking lot and playground. I went to Cheltenham High School in Elkins Park, it is gone now, also demolished, relocated to Wyncote. At Millersville State College my first dorm room was in Old Main – the building is gone. I worked at Drexel Tech, they changed the name to Drexel University, I spent 14 years at Spring Garden College – it went out of business. I was athletics director at Philadelphia College of Textiles & Science – they changed the name. As a disc jockey and sportscaster I worked at two FM stations – WiFi and WIBF, both gone. I worked for the Fleer Corporation for seven years and the ScoreBoard for one – both are now out of business.

People recognize that my life often revolved around sports and they ask me if I was a great athlete. Nope, in hindsight, I was probably not even a terribly good one. I was your average player who really loved sports, loved the competition, and loved the teamwork. I always wanted to play and, be there no doubt, I always played to win in sports and in life.

And as the clock ticks away on my lifetime I got to wondering how did all this happen? How did I end up in a career where a lot of it had to do with education, dealing with people and playing games and why was that so important? And then, thinking about it, I realized I was always being groomed – perhaps grooming myself - for all of this since I was just a very little guy.

The Glenside Kid

He was dressed all in black this small buckaroo
His cowboy hat had white trim, his holsters did too
Two cap-firing six guns were strapped to his side
A Firestone bike was his trusty ride

The times that he lived were incredibly real
His heroes were Rogers and Autry, even Bob Steele
Life was simple, exciting and free
He knew what a lucky young kid was he

His paper route provided him with cash
For the weekly Cowboy Matinee dash
School was important, life was sure fine
He had lots of friends to share this great time

The small cowboy is still riding that range
But finds today's world just a little bit strange
I-pods and cell phones and electronic crap
Are so overwhelming, he thinks he may snap

But looking back over a journey so fine
And reliving it all is life's sweet Valentine
And the little buckaroo, all dressed in black
Still longs for the day and sure wants to go back

- Ted Taylor

Chapter I – We're going to meet the twins

My youngest son Brett and his wife, Colleen, were expecting twins. It was February 2011 and very cold outside. She was going to have the babies this very day because the little boy was in the breach position and a c-section was on the agenda. We already knew, from the ultra sounds, that she was having one of each – and their names were already determined, Lily and Brett II.

We were on our way to the hospital to await their birth – my wife and I – and she reminded me that our youngest son Brett was always about family and now he was going to have one of his own.

Cindy said, "Do you remember what Brett said not so long ago?" He says a lot of things, I replied, and she countered, "No, he said now that you've written all those baseball books he'd like you to write one about you, about the stories you used to tell him as a kid and the columns you used to write in the newspaper."

I did remember. My growing up columns in the many papers I've written for – The Philadelphia Daily News, Willow Grove Guide, Public Spirit, Times Chronicle, Glenside News – always got enthusiastic responses, people like that stuff. Nostalgia is fun. I had kicked around the idea before – even started working on a book like this twice before - but it's not always that easy when the central figure in the effort is you.

She kept the conversation going and reminded me how much I loved the things Jean Shepherd wrote, especially his book "In God we Trust all others pay cash" and she said, "You've got a similar book lurking in you, why not write it?"

It got me to thinking that you need to know where you came from before you can understand exactly who you are. We are the sum of many parts, many people and many experiences. Those of us who grew up in the so-called "Baby Boomer" generation share many universal experiences so, in a way, I am writing this book about all of us.

The Glenside Kid

Playwright Edward Albee once wrote, "I write to find out what I am talking about", and I think that fits me like a glove. Author Rebecca West said, "I write books to find out things" and that was certainly the case in the baseball-themed books I've written.

I come from interesting families. At least I found them so. Maybe you will too – and maybe they'll remind you of your own families. I'm the American mongrel, no pure-bred stallion here. On my father's side I am "first generation" American. On my mother's side I am 'second generation". The Taylor family came from England; the Roth family came from Austria and Germany.

On the way to the hospital that day, travelling out Route 611 (Easton Road) we drove through Willow Grove past the shuttered Naval Air Base, Horsham, Warrington – a one time farming community that has exploded in to primer on how not to foster urban sprawl - and, finally, Doylestown an artsy crafty, yuppie haven that is also the Bucks County seat. Most of the trip was driven in a nasty wind swept rain storm – the c-section was scheduled for 1 PM - and it became clear to me we weren't going to be there by then. The rain caused delays and as we got closer we stopped and started our way through Doylestown's narrow streets. Finally we pulled in to the massive parking lot at the local hospital where our two latest grandchildren were about to make their debut.

Unlike our neighborhood hospital, amazingly, I found a free spot to park. Obviously this was going to be a good day. But it was already 1 PM; perhaps the babies were being born as we walked to the main entrance.

Chapter II - First there was Jack, then Helen, then me

My father was born in Manchester, Lancashire, England on Halloween 1905. He was the youngest of four Taylor children – Mary Sarah, Florence, John Joseph and him (Henry). Their Mom was Mary Ann Hill Taylor, their dad was John Taylor. In England John was a blacksmith and, later, a wheelwright. The family also evolved from the Goulden, English and Hill families according to ancient English marriage licenses and birth certificates that I found.

As the 19th Century drew to a close and despite the growing wealth due to trade and commerce, prosperity lay in the hands of very few of Manchester's residents. John Taylor wasn't one of the prosperous. Instead he was one of the working class people, who actually produced the wealth, yet the people like him lived, worked and often died in conditions of the most desperate poverty and degradation.

Innumerable reports and surveys were carried out during the late 19th century, and they all told much the same story: poor wages, impossibly long working hours, dangerous and unsanitary working conditions, even more unsanitary dwellings, little or no health provisions, high infant mortality and a short life expectancy. Is it any wonder that John wanted to get his wife and family out of there?

And on the subject of the United Kingdom's Taylor family, according to a woman from New Zealand who claims to be a distant relative, we (the John Taylor family) are, somehow, related to John Henry Taylor one of the "Triumvirate of Golf" – in other words one of professional golf's earliest stars. JHT also had humble beginnings, starting his golf career as a caddy. But perhaps that's true, my Dad was quite a good golfer and, when I played at it regularly, I could at least shoot par or be in the neighborhood.

One note of sadness enters the picture early on. The Taylor's had been in America less than a decade when eldest daughter Mary Sarah died, in 1918, (at age 19) of the flu. The influenza pandemic of 1918-1919 killed more people than World War I, at somewhere between 20 and 40 million people. It has been cited as the most devastating epidemic in recorded world history. More people died of influenza in a single year than in four-years of the Black Death Bubonic Plague from 1347 to 1351. Known as "Spanish Flu" or "La Grippe" the influenza of 1918-1919 was a global disaster. Our family was not spared. I wonder if my Grandparents had second thoughts that if they had they stayed in England, would she have avoided it? The answer, I believe, is probably not.

The SS Haverford, White Star Liner

Grandfather Taylor came to Philadelphia in 1910 – in steerage (the cheapest ticket) on the SS Haverford. The ship was built in 1899 by John Brown & Co. of Clydebank for the American Line. She was launched in 1901 and set out for her maiden voyage from Southampton to New York the same year. She was later assigned to several different routes including the American's Liverpool to Philadelphia service, the Red Star Line's Antwerp to New York route, and the Dominion Line's Liverpool-Halifax-Portland route. We still have his trunk with the White Star Line sticker on it.

He came to the United States by himself and would work for two years to earn enough money to bring the rest of the family over.

The Glenside Kid

He was 36 when he landed in Philadelphia and he reported for a job as sexton (a fancy word for janitor) at St. Martin-in-the-Fields Episcopal Church in the upper crust and historic Chestnut Hill section of Philadelphia. His church in England had pre-arranged the job for him. At first, according to family lore, he lived in a room in the church's basement. When the family came over they lived in a rented house on Highland Avenue within walking distance of the church. When they could afford to buy a home they relocated to 215 W. Mt. Pleasant Avenue in Mt. Airy. Years later when I was at Spring Garden College, and even now at Chestnut Hill College, I told people who asked "Yes, my Grandfather was associated with the church" and he was. He kept it neat and tidy and, according to a letter sent to my Grandmother upon his passing, loved maintaining the church.

English kids took to soccer like American kids did to baseball (and now football and basketball). Dad was a skilled soccer player and was recruited by Philadelphia's Northeast High School – then the city soccer powerhouse – to play for them. He also played for numerous semi-pro teams during the 1930's and my Mom often quipped that "he made more money playing soccer than he did at his job". Professional and amateur teams vied for the National Challenge Cup. Ethnic and regional leagues, such as the German American Football Association and Fall River Football Club, were the most vital sources for soccer in the 1930s, and most U.S. teams were composed largely of immigrants, like my father, from Scotland and England. Semi-pro was the way to go in those days, there really was no pro soccer in the United States. A picture of Dad with one of his teams hangs in my office. Sports always sports.

He was named Henry at birth, but disliked the name. Eventually he became known as Jack. Why? No one ever really told me. Even stranger, his brother was named John – Jack is usually the nickname for that – and yet he was always John or Johnny.

Jack was a dapper guy. Photos from the 20's and 30's show a self-assured and stylish young man who liked to dress well. He

The Glenside Kid

That's Jack sitting on the steps of the Taylor family vacation home in West Wildwood NJ. None of the seven young ladies in the picture are my mother.

seemed to be wearing white suits in a lot of the pictures, white shoes too. He was also a first class practical joker and some of the stories of his pranks are the stuff of legends. They tell me he always had a smile on his face and a laugh in his heart.

In addition to being a soccer star, Jack was a long-time Boy Scout (and later a Boy Scout leader), joined the U. S. Army as a member of the mounted cavalry (on his discharge it lists his horsemanship as "excellent") and, for a time, rode with the elite First City Troop of Philadelphia, a largely ceremonial unit of the Pennsylvania National Guard.

He was a Mason – Grand Master of the Michael Arnold Lodge in Philadelphia – and active in the church. He crammed a lot of living in to his short time on Earth. I never became a Mason, though I had opportunities. Had Dad lived I'm sure I'd have followed him there.

Uncle Harry, Aunt Mads & Aunt Bess Standing in front of the Roth family home on Limekiln Pike, Glenside, then a dirt road, circa 1900

My Mom, Helen Roth, was a child of privilege when she was born in 1909. She grew up the youngest of eight children in the suburbs and in the shadow of the William Welsh Harrison Estate, Grey Towers Castle (now at the hub of Arcadia University). Now Glenside, the area was called Harmer Hill when Phillip Roth and his parents (Karl and Katerina) settled there in the 1870's. The Roth family evolved from the Kohl's, Schupp's and Kalteneggers. Phillip was just 11 years old when his family emigrated here from Germany – the Civil War had been over for just nine years.

Helen graduated from Cheltenham High and Taylor Business School (how prophetic) and worked, first, for her father's leather goods company – C. F. Rumpf and Company of Philadelphia. The Roth family vacationed in Atlantic City each summer – staying at the ritzy Haddon Hall hotel, dining at the knife and Fork - and many photos remain of her escapades there. For reasons that fit in to the fact that no one in our family ever went by their correct first name, as a young lady she was known as "Sammi".

Photos of my mother as a girl - and young lady - show a striking beauty who had more than her share of beaus. She did all the things of the Roaring 20's and her scrapbooks show plays she

The Glenside Kid

attended in town, college functions she went to and it seemed that there was always something going on. Her boyfriends, according to the old photos, all seemed to have money and fancy cars. Somehow Jack Taylor came along and won her heart.

That's "Sammi" Roth on the right with best friend Bette Morrison. Note the "TS" on her swim suit, it stands for Taylor Business School. The photo is in Atlantic City. She's about 17.

Jack and Helen married on April 22, 1933 and, first, went to West Wildwood NJ where his parents owned a vacation home. After a week there, they left, by train, for their honeymoon in Niagara Falls. As the train departed the station John Taylor toppled to the platform, dead of a massive heart attack. It was May 4. They first learned of his death when they checked in to their hotel in Niagara Falls. Death has never been convenient – or even timely - in our family.

The Glenside Kid

The Roth Family Manse on Limekiln Pike, Glenside, Circa 1910

Mom's father, Phillip Ernest Roth, was a successful leather goods buyer and each winter, from November until March, he travelled throughout Europe buying product lines for his company to sell. The family legend also persists that Phillip, a very tall, handsome and dashing man, had a second family in Germany to go along with the one he had – including eight children – in Glenside. If so, World War II likely erased any records that existed. He was born in Berlin, Germany, which in 1871 had become the capital of the German Empire. The city was the economic center of the country and its' key rail hub. Even so, the elder Roth's, their eldest son, Phillip, and his younger brother, Henry, headed for the promise of the United States.

My Mother's Mother, Irma Kaltenegger, was born in Vienna, Austria in 1879 and came to the USA in 1904. At that time Vienna was the capital of a Habsburg empire that had become a political dinosaur in the world of industrial modernism. Its emperor, Franz Joseph, had come to power over fifty years earlier, following the revolutions of 1848, and he would rule for another sixteen years. In the two hundred years between 1700 and 1910, the population of Vienna grew by a factor of twenty, from a mere 123,000 to well

The Glenside Kid

over 2 million. Vienna was a vastly heterogeneous, multi-ethnic metropolis, made up of ethnic Germans, Hungarians, Czechs, Slovaks, Croats, Poles, Russians, Romanians, Italians, to name just the principal groups. It was a city wrought by political tensions. From 1897 to 1910 the city was governed by the highly popular (and populist) German nationalist, anti-Semitic mayor Karl Lueger.

That's Phillip Roth, third from left, and his wife Irma, second from left. Uncle George is center, back row. They're in Atlantic City, circa 1920. Fully dressed and on the beach. Imagine that.

When Phillip's first wife Lena (maiden name Kohl) died giving birth to their third daughter, Clara, he was left with six children. His quite elderly parents moved back in with him and helped to care for the children but, soon, he met, wooed and wed Irma - in 1907. Irma was 16 years younger than Phillip, taking on a large family at age 28. In 1908 she gave birth to Rudy and in 1909 my mother. Twins came the following year but were still born. The Rudy Roth cousins and I always used to laugh and say we were descended from a crazy woman. Irma had to be nuts to marry a much older man (he was 44) with six kids who was away from home four-or-five months every year. On the other hand, as it has been pointed out, for his day, Phillip was considered "well off".

When Grand pop Roth died in 1926 his eldest son Harry took over his job and stayed with it well in to the 1960's. It was on a trip in 1955 to New York see Uncle Harry off when I first boarded the most magnificent ocean liner in the world – The S S United States. It was actually a trip we took each November to see him off and it always started with lunch on a luxury liner, a show at Radio City Music Hall and a nice train ride home. It's the stuff you remember, the things that help shape you. Every time I drive past the rusty hulk of that magnificent ship in South Philadelphia I recall a greater time for it and hope, one day, some one restores it.

      The Roth's are pretty much all gone now. Only two of the eight children had male heirs – Harry Roth (had Tom) and Rudy Roth (had George). If you want to stop by and say hi to Phillip and Irma, they're in Roslyn PA's Hillside Cemetery.

Chapter III - By the sea

We were awaiting the babies – heck we hadn't even left Colleen's room yet, when Brett, ever the realist, said, "Dad, I'm glad you and Mom have the place at the shore, at least the kids will have someplace to go that we can afford for our vacation".

And, of course, he did, as do all our kids and grandkids. We bought our seashore home in Wildwood Crest in 2000 and have enjoyed every moment of its ownership. Not only do we have a better social life there – and closer friends like Emerson and Sharon Shaw, Gene and Diane Bonetti, Will and Ann Wanamaker – we also are able to entertain family and friends there whenever we wish.

It's funny that we ended up in Wildwood Crest because that town has played a recurrent role in our family history. In fact one of the oldest relics we have from Grandmother Roth was a small red glass cup that reads "Wildwood, Irma, 1905" on it.

Wildwood was originally incorporated as a borough by an Act of the New Jersey Legislature on May 1, 1895, from portions of Middle Township, based on the results of a referendum held the previous day. The Wildwoods actually began developing as a resort in the last decade of the 19th century. On January 1, 1912, Wildwood was incorporated as a city, replacing both Wildwood borough and Holly Beach City.

Sometime in the early 1920's the Taylor's – John and Mary Ann – purchased a cottage in West Wildwood which is one of the four communities that comprise the Greater Wildwood resort. Family pictures show the one-story house and recurrent gatherings of young people though we don't have an actual street address and efforts to find the place in recent years have failed. The cottage is probably long demolished.

A building boom began in the 1950's in the Wildwoods, due partially to the construction and completion of the Garden State Parkway. My personal boyhood memories are of the Wildwood boardwalk and two amusements that some say I hallucinated. One was an arcade where you threw baseballs at a hole in the wall and if it went in a little pig came sailing down a slide, ran around an enclosed area – oinking as it went – and then back in to wherever it came from. The other was of an enclosure that featured race cars driven by monkeys.

By the mid-40's my father had enough of West Wildwood. Nanny (Mary Ann) Taylor would give him a list of things to fix the minute we arrived and his "vacation" would be spent repairing the place so Nanny could rent it.

Wildwood's most notable features are its beach – usually ranked the best in the state - and 1.8 miles of boardwalk, home to the Morey's Piers amusement complex and water parks owned by Morey's Piers. The boardwalk is said to feature more amusement attractions that Disney World and features a trolley called the "Tramcar, which runs from end to end. In June 2006, its Doo-Wop-style motels were placed on the National Trust for Historic Preservation's annual Eleven Most Endangered List, described as "irreplaceable icons of popular culture."

"Rock Around the Clock", which is often credited as the first rock and roll record, was first performed on Memorial Day weekend in 1954 at the HofBrau Hotel in Wildwood by Bill Haley & His Comets. The song's status as one of the first rock and roll hits has given rise to the city's claim as "the birthplace of rock and roll". I remember one summer sitting on the beach in Ocean City when my teenaged cousin Doris Jenkins told me that she and her boyfriend had just been to Wildwood to see "this rock 'n roll guy, Bill Haley". Annual tribute concerts to the music legacy of the 1950's and 60's usually sell out at the city's spacious Convention Center. The city had so many name entertainers performing there in the 50's that it actually earned the title "Las Vegas of the East".

By 1946 the Jack Taylor family was no longer vacationing in Wildwood, but rather in Ocean City, known as "America's Family Resort"

The Glenside Kid

Chapter IV - The Kid gets cooked, as does Dad's Goose

Ocean City, NJ, played a huge role in my life from about age six until I was ready for college – and even well beyond. Cindy and I actually owned a home there during the 1980's when I worked, summers, for the city recreation department, ran a summer camp and coached a kid's baseball team.

The resort town known as "America's Family Resort" is among the most vivid of my childhood memories and as a young boy I knew that the vacation actually started when we hit the traffic circle in Somers Point and then navigated "The causeway" in to town. The first landmark was *Hogates* a real nice seafood restaurant and right next to it was *Chris's* another restaurant – both annual family dining favorites. Both long gone now.

Once you passed those two icons of the summer it was downhill on Ninth Street for a few blocks – past the fire house with the large and interesting goldfish display and city hall – on to Central Avenue, where it intersected with Ninth, where we would spend our vacation.

The place where we stayed each summer was actually right next to Ocean City High School. It was a three-story white clapboard home, windows and trimming in ocean blue, called *"The Longshore Guest House"* and it was owned by the Snyder family.

It was really a typical seashore rooming house and the family (Me, Mom and Dad) took a room – usually the same one - there for our vacation. As I recall we'd stay for two weeks. You couldn't cook in your room – it was just a double bed for them, a cot for me and a couple of bureaus, so we took our breakfast at the *Chatterbox* which was on the opposite corner and often ate dinner at *The Strand Hotel* which was right down the street. Lunch was usually a hot dog grabbed from a stand on the board walk. Dad parked the '40 Plymouth in front of the building when we got there and didn't drive too many places once we settled in.

The Glenside Kid

The exceptions would be when it rained and we headed to Atlantic City for a day at *The Steel Pier* to catch the high diving horse, some first run movies and other amusements, or if we decided to go fishing. Otherwise we could walk almost anywhere we wanted to go – the beach, the boardwalk, for meals.

The elderly (at least to me) woman who owned the place was called "Grandma Snyder" by everyone. (I don't think that I ever knew her first name.) She was an extra grandmother – the one I had at the shore. Her son was named Billy and he was a life guard and her daughter was named Peggy – she was a teenager and acted as a surrogate big sister for me when Mom and Dad went out in the evening and I needed babysitting.

One of my favorite boardwalk haunts was always the Penny Arcade. It was owned, then, by the Bingham Family and it had neat rides, skee ball – at which I excelled - and vending machines that, for a penny, rewarded you with postcard sized pictures of cowboys, movie actors and athletes. We spent a lot of time at Bingham's. I had a lot of Exhibit cards – including the risqué' pin up girl ones that I hid in the bottom of my sock drawer.

Nearby was the *Flanders Hotel* and that was right on the boardwalk – and it had this nifty ocean-water-filled swimming pool. On one side of the boardwalk was the hotel and the pool and on the other was the beach and the ocean. Being well off was kind of a pre-requisite to staying there, Mom's friend Mildred and her family did. We weren't and we didn't. The Taylor's stayed at *The Longshore*.

The Glenside Kid

My father and I sample the Ocean City surf.
Was I doing what it looks like I was doing?

It's 1946, I'm almost six, and one day, mid-vacation, my Dad decided that he would take me fishing. Mom was going to enjoy a day of boardwalk and Asbury Avenue shopping by herself. We got up early, my mother was sound asleep. Got dressed, grabbed a quick breakfast at the restaurant, hopped in the car and headed for the bay.

Dad decided we'd be better off just going out by ourselves, rather than in one of those half-day deep sea fishing boats. He rented a small boat with an outboard motor, rented me a fishing pole - Dad had his own fishing gear - bought the bait and we shoved off.

The Ocean City Causeway, it meant you were there for your great vacation. How lucky were you?

The Glenside Kid

To get to the best fishing spots you had to go under the drawbridge and causeway – that was cool, watching the cars pass over you - and out past 34th Street. There were lots of boats in the water that day – just like most summer days. I would watch the cars coming in imagining that they were arriving for their vacations too. Weren't we all just the luckiest people in the world?

The sun came up hot, it was getting warm, and before long I took off my shorts – I had bathing trunks on under them – and my tee shirt. And that's the way I was in the boat as the day progressed. No hat, no nothing. And needless to say not only did we catch a few fish I caught a terrible case of sun burn. I'm little, what do I know? Dad must have been daydreaming too and it never occurred to him that I was being toasted alive.

Finally, we headed back to the dock and I was feeling, well, a little uncomfortable. Not really sick, but not really good either. My skin hurt, even my hair hurt. Dad had me put my shirt and shorts back on before we got off the boat but the damage was done.

By the time we got to Grandma Snyder's I was, to be charitable, redder than a $25 lobster. Actually I was starting to feel really awful. Dad decided that I should take a nap – and I did. I went out like a light.

Mom came home, saw me sleeping and asked Dad how we did. "We did swell, I gave the fish we caught to Mrs. Snyder," he said. He didn't mention my condition – and Mom didn't notice.

Dinner time rolled around and Dad suggested we walk over to the *Strand Hotel*. Again, Mom failed to notice how red I was. I got dressed while Dad distracted her. Putting on clothes, even shorts, was brutal. Needless to say, I wasn't terribly hungry but I had to help Dad pull this off.

But once we hit the restaurant and were seated it dawned on her that I was a lot redder than your average six-year-old. Her Teutonic temper flared, "What did you do to Teddy?" she shrieked.

The Glenside Kid

Poor Dad, he had no defenses. But he, being an Englishman, didn't let the lack of a defensible position keep him from a good argument.

Me, I felt like crap, and here were my parents – now the center of everyone's attention – yelling at the top of their lungs at each other. Finally Dad did the only thing left for him to do; he stomped out of the restaurant.

My Mom looked at me and said "follow him and tell him to come back here this instant". Follow him? I could hardly walk. Was she nuts? But off I toddled and caught Dad at the *Longshore*. Where else was he going to go? Mrs. Snyder saw me and said, as I recall, "Oh my God" and the next thing you knew I was in a bathtub in her living quarters and they were pouring tea on me. I was, literally, bathing in tea – and, you know what, it took the sting right out of the sunburn. A lemon, some ice, a little sugar and I'd have been a cool summer drink.

I didn't go to the beach for a few days and, as I remember it, wore long sleeves and long pants as well as a hat (probably an A's hat, Dad was an A's fan).

Mom and Dad communicated through me, "Tell your father that I think we should go to the boardwalk today" or "Tell your mother I was planning to take a drive to Atlantic City". It wasn't all that much fun.

But I survived – as did their marriage.

When Dad died in June, 1949, Mrs. Snyder invited Mom and me to come to the shore as her guests for a couple of weeks – and we did. We actually stayed with her in her apartment, just like family. I was only little at the time, but I remember how kind everyone was to us with dad's passing.

But I still laugh when I recall that Mom almost killed him three years before that when he let me get cooked in a boat in the bay.

The next summer Aunt Mads (Madeline) Jenkins rented an entire rooming house and then, in turn, rented the rooms to vacationers. She always wanted to be a real estate mogul. My aunt invited Mom and me to stay for a week and when we got there she showed us to a very nice room. We were no sooner unpacked when she arrived at the door and said, "I'm sorry, I just rented this room." Mom slept on the couch in Mads' apartment, I slept on the floor. We went home after two days.

From 1950 until Mom married Ernie our seashore "vacations" were pretty much limited to day trips or a day or two bunking with one of her friends or some other relative.

In the Summer of 1956 the four of us (Mom, Dad, Sister Pat and me) rented a nice first floor duplex at 16th and Asbury and spent two glorious weeks there. We repeated that vacation in 1957 and 1958.

As an older teenager I would go to Ocean City with my friends for long weekends. There was one place where we stayed, the Wesley Arms, that a room cost just $5-a-night. That was if you didn't mind the fact that it had no door. If you wanted one with a door it was $10.

Ocean City was a favorite – and it was the destination of lots of our friends for many years. Sometimes I really miss it.

The Glenside Kid

Chapter V – What is it about celebrities?

The c-section was originally due at 1 PM. When we got there the nurse at the desk in the maternity section said "You can go in and see her if you want, there will be a delay. It seems like we're having a run of natural births today." Oh goodie, I thought, I hate hospitals as it is and now it looks like I'm going to be here for awhile.

My daughter, Melissa, her husband Jeff and two kids – Brittany and Bailey - soon arrived. "Hey Dad isn't there anything you can do to speed things up, you're kind of a local celebrity." But the truth was there was nothing I could do. The Good Lord- and the doctor – were in charge here. Babies know nothing about celebrities.

What's a celebrity anyway? My kids think I was one because I've written books, had my own radio shows, been on TV. But, really, I'm just me. And it was certain that Colleen's doctor could care less how many books I've written and likely never heard me on the radio or saw me on TV.

But it got me thinking. I have met countless celebrities in my life. I've been in the company of two U. S. Presidents – Ronald Reagan and George W. Bush, and stood near two others John F. Kennedy and Harry Truman – and countless Senators and Congressmen. I've met actors and actresses, playwrights and authors.

As my life has unfolded, I have found that celebrities are pretty much just regular people whom fame, for some reason, has touched. Most of the celebrities I have met have been decent people. Some sports-related ones, like Rich Ashburn, Robin Roberts, Del Ennis, Gus Zernial, Ferris Fain, Bobby Shantz, Clyde Drexler, Reggie White, Steve Young and Tommy Glavine have been beyond nice.

The Glenside Kid

As a kid my Mom took me to the Arthur Godfrey radio show in New York City. I met Mr. Godfrey and was impressed. He was, at that time, one of the biggest stars in broadcasting. He walked in to the studio, a stocky, red-haired man who was wearing a flannel shirt, khaki pants and moccasins. It was, of course, the radio and no one apparently dressed up to be on it. Certainly not Arthur Godfrey.. I wanted a career in radio as a result of that meeting and dabbled in it for over two decades. As a teenager I bought a Sears Silvertone reel-to-reel tape recorder and taped mock radio shows on it. I kept the Gerhard sister's record store in Glenside solvent for years, buying hit records as they came out.

Joe Niagara, a top radio deejay on WIBG in Philly as "The Rockin' Bird" when I was growing up, became a friend later in life when I was doing my weekly radio show in one studio (for WIBF FM) and in the adjacent one Joe was taping his weekly Channel 29 TV show.

George W. Bush was the owner of the Texas Rangers baseball team when I met him at the baseball winter meetings in 1992 in Louisville KY and we talked baseball for almost an hour. I liked the man. On an impulse I got him and his friend Peter O'Malley (then the owner of the Los Angeles Dodgers) to sign a baseball for me. It sits next to the one signed for me by his father George H. W. Bush on a shelf in my rec room.

I believe that President Reagan was the greatest president of my lifetime and I met him after his Presidency when I was a college Athletics Director and he was the guest speaker at an NCAA awards dinner.

Harry S Truman and Franklin D. Roosevelt are also pretty high in my estimation as well and when I tell my college students that, though I am a lifelong Republican, two of my favorite three Presidents' were Democrats they are amazed. (Most college professors are liberals, I am the exception – perhaps the only one at Chestnut Hill.)

The Glenside Kid

Harry's "The Buck Stops Here" motto became my own personal mantra. When I was a small boy our Glenside School teacher took us to the grand 30th Street Station in Philadelphia so we could see President Truman's whistle-stop campaign first hand – it was 1948. I saw him and I was hooked on politics. I was in center city Philadelphia in 1960 when John F. Kennedy was giving a speech from the back of a car and I walked right up to him and said "hi". He smiled, I'll bet he didn't know I wasn't old enough to vote.

As a kid I was influenced to be a teacher by Florence Johannes and Charlotte Roatche at Glenside School, Phil Finkeldey and J. Hamilton Lampe at Thomas Williams Junior High and Dave Harr and George Stabley at Cheltenham High. They made learning magic. In my years as a teacher and, later, college professor I have tried to emulate and replicate the excitement they brought to a classroom.

Jean Shepherd always inspired me to be a writer. I was in Shep's company several times. He was a unique individual – with such a fertile mind - and never appreciated as he should have been. But you always remember the 'first" of anything and my first brush with real live celebrities happened in the unlikely location of Bath, NY.

Chapter VI – We meet the Sons of the Pioneers

As a kid I loved cowboys. Every Saturday my pals and I from the neighborhood would go to either one of the two movie theatres in our area. The Glenside or the Keswick for a matinee – that meant a cartoon, Movie Tone news, an episode of a serial and a cowboy picture. When the star was Roy Rogers I was even more excited. I loved Roy and his whole crew – Dale Evans, Gabby Hayes, Pat Brady, Bob Nolan and The Sons of the Pioneers singing group and, of course, Trigger the horse.

The magnificent Keswick Theatre, the Kid's window on the world of true adventure

The Keswick Theatre first opened its doors on Christmas Night, 1928. Nationally recognized as the most comfortable, acoustically perfect listening room in the entire Philadelphia market, the Keswick was designed by acclaimed architect Horace Trumbauer (who also created the Phila. Museum of Art). Initially a combination vaudeville/movie house, the Keswick hosted such legends as Stepin' Fetchit, Paul Robeson and Ina Ray Hutton (Betty's sister) with her all-girl band. In 1955, the theater was remodeled into a cinemascope film house, hosting the area's

The Glenside Kid

premiere releases of most of the big-budget movies of the 1950s and '60s.

Today the Keswick is one of the top showplaces in the Delaware Valley for entertainment acts. Larry O'Brien, the leader of the *Glenn Miller Orchestra*, once called the Keswick a theatre "with almost perfect acoustics". The Glenside Theatre, on the other hand, is now an office building, I guess the acoustics there weren't so hot.

My Dad would also take me to other movie houses when a Roy Rogers feature was playing – sometimes to Hatboro, sometimes to "The Grove" Willow Grove, the "Yorktown" in Elkins Park or maybe to the "Hiway" Theatre in Jenkintown. All gone now except the Hiway. I couldn't get enough of cowboys. I had all their records (78 RPM, by the way), books and comics, even trading cards. Both the Roy Rogers and Gene Autry Rodeos played at the Arena in West Philly every year and it was a certainty that I'd be there too. Dad made sure of it.

I had all the gear, a two Texan brand cap gun and holster set, a very cool black hat and several shirts that had Roy Rogers on them or were designed like those Roy used to wear. The one thing I didn't ever have was a pair of cowboy boots. I had something called "low arches" in my feet and our doctor said I shouldn't wear cowboy boots. Mom stood firm on that. It was a bummer and I've never owned a pair of cowboy boots in my life.

We'd go to the matinees every Saturday and then, on the way home, we'd replay the whole movie in our own kid-like way. I had good looking cowboy stuff – thanks to my parents - so I was usually the one playing the hero guy. I liked that.

The Magical Trip to Canada

It's the summer of 1947 and two years before my father passed away of cancer. He was already ill from the disease that would take his life but was still working for De Long Hook & Eye in Philadelphia. His boss sent him on a business trip and he drove the family's 1940 Plymouth to the DeLong plant in Ontario, Canada for reasons that are lost to me – and to time. In any event it turned out to be our last family vacation – me, Mom and Dad.

Maybe he knew what was coming and wanted to share what time he had left with us, I don't really know. But I wouldn't be surprised if that wasn't what motivated him. I do know that he had been in and out of Temple Hospital for at least the two years leading up to that time.

We took off for Ontario and the first night on the road we stayed in a large hotel in the coal region of Pennsylvania, in downtown Scranton. I can't tell you the name of the hotel, but our room was higher above the street than any place that I had ever slept before. The honking horns below kept me awake, but it was exciting. To me Scranton was a big city.

The next day we drove as far as the town of Bath in upper New York State. We checked in to a tourist home for the night – motels were not yet a viable option - and then went in to the town, such as it was, for dinner. We ended up at White's Restaurant which, according to their placemat, was 134 miles from Niagara Falls, 22 miles from Corning and 68 miles from Rochester.

As we were eating dinner I noticed three good-looking men walk in the door. It was New York State but these guys looked like real cowboys. They each wore Stetson hats, had tooled leather boots, a big buckle on their belts and fancy Cowboy shirts. They sure looked familiar, but how would I know anyone in Bath, NY? The more I stared at them the more familiar they looked. Maybe it was because they had on the western gear, but darn it I just know that I knew them.

Then the light bulb in my little buckaroo brain came on…"They are the Sons of the Pioneers", I thought and I whispered that to my father. He smiled and said, "What would they be doing up here?" And I had to admit that was a really good question. This was not the wild west, it was up-state New York for crying out loud.

The Glenside Kid

But then Dad turned to my Mom and said, "You know Helen, they really do look like the Sons of the Pioneers." Thanks to me and our movie sojourns Dad also knew his cowboys.

Sons of the Pioneers 1947, Clockwise: Bob Nolan, Karl Farr, Lloyd Perryman, Tim Spencer, Hugh Farr & Pat Brady

That was all I needed to hear. I grabbed my placemat, got up from our table and walked over to the three men. I was very polite, introduced myself, and asked "Are you the Sons of the Pioneers?" and one of them, Karl Farr, I think, said "We're some of them". Oh my God! I had hit pay dirt. I was talking to the very guys who talked to Roy Rogers.

Before I could say "Round up time in Texas" the three men – Farr, Lloyd Perryman and Pat Brady had all signed the placemat for me. Pat even wrote "Best of happiness Teddy" before his name, Farr wished me "Best of luck" and Perryman added "Here's my best". I had died and gone to Heaven.

It turns out that the three of them were doing an appearance – with the other band members, back at the hotel - at a local theatre and were just grabbing a bite to eat before heading off to sing. Why we didn't go, I don't know, but it was just the coolest thing that ever happened to me in my young life. The vacation was now a success regardless of what happened the rest of the time.

We did go to Niagara Falls on the way to Ontario – it was where my parents had spent their Honeymoon, such as it was, when they were first married. We rode the "Maid of the Mist" and ooh'ed and aahh'ed about the falls. They were the most awesome thing this little guy had ever seen.

I still have that placement and all the wonderful memories of a kid and his family meeting some of the heroes of my young life. It's also one of the precious memories I have of my Dad, and it is so vivid.

Chapter VII – We drive the Benz to the hospital

My eldest son Chris and his wife Lisa walked in the hospital waiting room. "Any word on the babies?" he asked. We muttered "no" and we've been waiting for quite a while. Our patience was ebbing. At least mine was. I dislike waiting for anything – even new grandchildren.

"We saw the Benz out in the lot," he said, "I drove my GTO here." Both cars, my Benz and his GTO are our "toys". They stay garaged and mostly off the road. My Cabernet Red 1999 500 SL Mercedes Benz cost $95,000+ new – my first three homes combined didn't cost that much.

Chris, like me, has a passion for cars. Cars have always been important to both of us. He buys a new one, and then I buy a new one. My wife just shrugs. "You two have this goofy 'car thing'", she says and lets it go at that.

Chris's first car was an old Nash Rambler that had more "Bondo" on its' body than metal. We dubbed it "The Flintstone Mobile" and I called him "James Bondo". He drove it to Florida after he graduated from high school. How it made it defies logic or reason. My first car was a 1950 Ford, a great car.

In real life – and to the college where I teach – I drive my Ford Taurus SEL. My wife drives a Kia Sorrento. Not pretentious, but nice cars. The Benz is my pretentious one. I save it for weekends at the shore and special events.

The first car of family importance that I remember as a kid was the family's gray 1940 Plymouth. They tell me it was preceded by a 1928 Ford Model T, but that car provides no memories for me.

But the '40 Plymouth was always there. It took me from little kid to teenager. It also took me to the movies, to dances, to the ball game. It provided the wheels of my childhood.

Chapter VIII - The 1940 Plymouth

We lived in a twin house on a one block long street in Glenside named Oak Road – and the only Oak tree on the block was in our front yard. It was a big darn tree and shed a ton of leaves every fall. The squirrels that resided in the tree would frequently conk you on the head with acorns if you weren't careful. We had lived at 338 Oak Road since 1941 when my father sold his brand new '41 Ford (quite reluctantly, I'm told) and the house we lived in on Sedgewick Street in Mt. Airy so that he could pull together enough money to return my Mom to her old Glenside neighborhood. The town is like that, it gets in your blood. It was certainly in hers. It was hard getting her to leave – and then it was only to Abington.

The reason Mom wanted to come back was that her sister Clare (Clara, actually) lived on Oak Road with her husband Charlie and two kids – Buddy (Charles Jr.) and Barbara. The Sines kids were older than me and, in many ways, soon became like my big sister and bigger brother. Buddy was a blonde haired boy, Barbara had dark hair – they were both good looking kids. When the house at 338 went up for sale my father had no choice it was move to Glenside or, well, he didn't want to find out the alternative. For example he had been a life-long Episcopalian when they married and before he knew what hit him he was Presbyterian. Why? Mom was Presbyterian and that was reason enough. My dad chose his battles carefully, I'm told.

The move also coincided with the beginnings of World War II and that meant that cars were scarce. Dad was already an Army veteran and just old enough to not be called back in to the service. He did, however, become our neighborhood Air Raid Warden. I remember his sparkling white helmet and the black pull down shades so that when the Germans flew over and bombed us they wouldn't be able to see our house lights. It must have worked, Glenside was never bombed.

The Glenside Kid

Barbara Sines was my cousin, and the "big sister" I never had

Dad's first new car, and the one he sacrificed to move to Glenside, was a 1941 Super De Luxe Ford – the best model that year. Obviously he liked cars too. These babies were much more modern with a wide body that nearly covered the running boards. The front and rear fenders were still pronounced as in earlier models, but were integrated more into the body. The headlights were pushed all the way up and out over the front wheels. The 1941 grille was a three-part affair with a tall center section bookended by twin kidneys low on the fenders and vertical bars all around. When I go to vintage car shows I always look for a '41 Ford and wonder if, maybe, it once belonged to my Dad.

But buying the new house meant selling his new car. Dad still needed wheels to get to work each day so he bought a black 1928 Model T Ford –it was a real clunker, I'm told. Once, when we were going to the shore, the old buggy broke down on the Tacony Palmyra Bridge. Dad got out with a ping pong paddle, whacked the carburetor a few times, and it came back to life. The term for that, I believe, is percussive maintenance.

1940 Plymouth 4-door

The Model T lasted through the war years and when it was over new ones were still very hard to get. In fact if you wanted one you went on a waiting list. Early in 1947 a friend of my father's hit the top of such a list and sold him his 1940 Plymouth – a major step up from the Model T. It was gray and had a ship – *The Mayflower*, I think – as a hood ornament. It also had the Scott (auto dealer) sailboat logo on the trunk, and I still see that logo to this day on cars.

We kept that car well in to the mid-1950's. It ran like a top and my Mom would drive it anywhere. In some ways it was also like a tank. Once I recall she picked me up at junior high school in a blizzard and, while all the newer cars were sliding all over the place, our big, old, quite heavy car – equipped with tire chains - just blazed a trail through the snow from Wyncote to our Glenside home. When it came to driving Mom was fearless.

Cars have always fascinated me. My first one was a stick-shift, V-8, green 1950 Ford, which like your first girlfriend, is something you will never forget. My new father, the former Uncle Ernie, gave it to me when I turned 16. It took me 20 days to get my driver's license. Following that my next car was a 1954 Ford Crestline – black-and-white exterior, coral interior, very sharp. I had really moved up in class, this number had leather seats and windows that rolled down in to the side panels – it was called a hard-top convertible, even though it didn't actually convert. I got it because Ernie got a new 1957 Mercury Phaeton.

I soon went to college – and you couldn't have a car as a freshman at Millersville – so we sold the '54 Ford to Ernie's friend Joe Bates – it was August, 1958. Two weeks later the transmission fell out. Whoops. Joe's kid was kinda hard on the car, I guess. Someone said he was drag racing when it happened. Since Pop was Joe's boss nothing ever came of it – like him paying for a new transmission.

One weekend home, late in my freshman year I bought a 1951 metallic green Pontiac off a used car lot owned by a friend's uncle. It, too, was like a tank. Once, when I drove through a driving rain storm on my way to visit a buddy in Ocean City NJ, my brakes failed and when I got there I had to down shift it to stop, nudging it against an Oak tree to complete the stop. The next day the brakes were dry and I was good to go.

My first new car was a 1960 Chevrolet Biscayne. I bought it at George W. Coupe Chevrolet in Glenside. I loved having a new car. My friend Merritt Sticker's Mother bought him a bright red, fully loaded, 1960 Impala – which was nothing short of regal – but mine was special because I bought it for me with my own money.

Pop had a 1958 Cadillac that he bought the year after he bought the 1957 Mercury. The Mercury was a very fancy car, but it got wrecked on the way home from a service call at the place where he bought it over in Jenkintown. What happened was that a car load of Catholic Priests – on the way to a golf match – ran a stop sign and hit him broadside. Lucky for us, we were Presbyterians. The priests called another car and continued on to the golf course. Pop survived and they put the Mercury back together but it was never right and he ditched it after a year. I actually took Ginny to my senior prom at the Meadowlands Country Club in his new Caddy. I was hot stuff.

In my lifetime I had a run of Caddy's myself. Once I bought a two-door white one, the model was the Calais that had a sticker in the back window that said "Italian American Civil Rights League". My wife, Cindy, was an Italian from South Philly and asked a friend of hers what that sticker meant and she laughed and said, "It means you can park any place you damn well please in South Philly." I kept the sticker on the car and parked it anywhere I damn well pleased.

When Cadillac ceased being the luxury car it had always been – American cars generally went in to decline with the influx of the new foreign models - I became a Mercedes Benz guy and have had six of them so far. Currently I own a red 500SL convertible.

But, really, I've had so many different cars in my lifetime I've lost track of them. I doubt I could recall them all even if I wanted to. There were Fords, Chevys, a few Pontiacs, a Toyota that son Chris totaled against a tree, a Jeep Cherokee that was the worst car I ever owned and a P T Cruiser convertible that, on the day I bought it, promised it to my grand daughter Brittany and delivered it to her in her senior year of high school.

Our kids all had a variety of different cars and when he was a teenager, we bought son Brett a Yugo – arguably the worst car ever assembled and dubbed by many as "the worst car of the millennium". We kept trying to get rid of it, it kept coming back. Brett was driving it on the 309 Expressway in Montgomeryville one day when the engine caught fire. Other reports of how bad the car really was included one guy saying the fastest he could get his to go was 42 MPH and when it hit that speed it sounded just like a blender on purée. Still another reported reaching out to turn on his radio and when he did so it fell out of the dashboard and on to the floor of the car. Suffice it to say, Brett has never forgotten his first car either.

The Glenside Kid

Chapter IX - Bored to death in the waiting room.

We waited and waited for the twins to arrive. For a modern suburban hospital in this very affluent town the waiting room was just this side of dingy Why beat around the bush? It was a dump. Lots of uncomfortable chairs jammed in together. An oil painting of somebody in a Doctor's jacket hung askew from the wall and where the name plate once was somebody had stuck a white label. The poor guy was obviously a onetime big shot at the hospital, now his likeness hangs in, what looked like, a thrift store wood-peeling frame, with a label for a name plate. Classy. Not at all.

The TV, such as it was in the room, offered little escape for us. ESPN was carrying a basketball game that no one cared about and there was something else on about dogs. Daytime TV, as a rule, sucks. The channels available in most hospitals make you wish you were someplace else. Maybe that's intentional.

TV, in our age, usually has so many sports events on the air that we have grown numb to them. In the waiting room I was growing numb trying to make sense of why we were still waiting.

At 3.30 my wife's cell phone rang. She glanced down, "It's Brett," she said. I wondered why he was calling us. He told her that Colleen hadn't gone in to the delivery room yet. I wasn't thrilled.   I wished I was at, perhaps, a ball game.

At about 3.45 Brett comes running in to the waiting room and announces "the twin have arrived and they are beautiful". Prejudiced? Of course, but he was right they were really something.

He led us to the nursery where little Brett II and Lily (she beat him out by 30 seconds making her, eternally, his older sister) were both getting cleaned up and ready for their debuts.

Little Lily displayed her powerful lungs and you could hear her all over the maternity wing. Brett II just kind of laid there and took it all in. She was vocal, he was curious.

The Glenside Kid

She was dainty with a little girl look. He looked like a boy." *He'll be able to take care of himself,"* Cindy said, *"and maybe he'll be your athlete."* I hoped, at least, he'd be a sports fan.

To this day I enjoy going to see live sports. I have attended seven Super Bowls, a half dozen baseball All-Star games, a like number of All-Star NBA games and countless Phillies games in recent years. I was in Veteran's Stadium, the hometown ballpark, in 1980 when the Phillies won their first-ever World's Championship. As a kid I saw as many A's games as Phillies games, because my family preferred Mr. Mack's Athletics.

For football I loved the college game most of all. I enjoyed the marching bands, the pageantry, the color, the excitement generated by the students and alumni. Saturday on a college campus attending a football game was, to me, as good as it got. Every fall we still catch at least one college football game – usually "Homecoming" weekend at Millersville where the Marauders regularly get their doors blown off. Who schedules these slaughters anyway? It would so much more fun if they'd win one every so often.

My next door neighbor in Glenside when I was a kid, Dr. Ernest Harting, was a professor at Temple University with season 50-yard-line tickets that he never used. As a consequence I attended just about every Temple home football game in the decade of the 1950's – though the Owls were pretty dreadful during that decade. I'm sure I saw Bill Cosby play for Temple but even he will admit that the teams he played for were, generally, awful. They two memorable coaches – Al Kawal (I always referred to him as Al Cohol) and Josh Cody who appeared to be old enough to be Buffalo Bill Cody's brother.

The University of Pennsylvania's games were my favorites. Huge crowds flocked to see the pre-Ivy league Quakers take on – and often beat - the best teams in the country. This was the college that spawned great pros – Chuck Bednarik, Angelo Musi, Frank X. Reagan – and then it went Ivy and all the fun and most of the fans

The Glenside Kid

departed. While in high school I took a job as an usher at Franklin Field just so I'd get to see the Penn games for free. They would draw 60,000-or-more fans to every game. To this day I consider myself a "subway alumnus" of Penn.

Ironically, the first live football game I ever attended was the 1948 NFL Championship at Shibe Park in Philly. Later in life I would attend seven Super Bowls, but, sadly, the Eagles never were a part of the equation.

The Glenside Kid

Chapter X - An Eagles Game with Uncle Charlie

It's December 19, 1948 just six days until Christmas. It was snowing; you'll pardon the expression, like a son-of-a-bitch. On that day my Uncle Charlie Sines called my Mom and wondered if I'd like to accompany him to the Eagles-Chicago Cardinals NFL Championship game. It was a blizzard out, pure and simple.

My Dad was quite ill, he was in and out of the hospital and, honestly, I don't recall if he was even home for that last Christmas. I suppose he was, but Mom was always going back-and-forth to Temple Hospital where he was being treated. Sometimes I'd go along, but had to wait outside his room – kids weren't allowed in. Why? Somebody's dumb rule, I guess.

My various uncles had started stepping up and began playing surrogate father to me. Apparently everyone knew that my father's days were numbered. Unlike Uncle Ernie, Uncle Charlie scared the crap out of me. I was afraid of him and I have no idea why, except for the fact he was big, going bald and quite gruff, I suppose.

One classic Uncle Charlie story that will help you understand this man happened on a Mischief Night sometime in the early 50's. His hunting dog, Missy, had escaped from the backyard kennel where he kept her and he was looking up and down Oak road for the errant pooch. As he was out in the neighborhood looking the Cheltenham police swooped down on a bunch of mischief making kids – including Uncle Charlie's son Buddy. As Uncle Charlie walked by the cops were putting Buddy in to the back of a squad car. "Hey Dad can't you help me out here?" Buddy wailed. His father shot him a dirty look and said, "You got in to the mess, you get out of it. I'm looking for my dog." My Aunt Clare had to go to the police station to spring Buddy. Uncle Charlie later found the dog.

A couple of other things you need to know about Uncle Charlie. He was a rough hewn man who started his working life driving a steam shovel at a quarry and, eventually, bought the quarry

The Glenside Kid

in Glenside. That big hole in the ground made him a wealthy man and he had time for the real passion in his life – golf.

It was on the links of Lu Lu Temple Country Club in Glenside that Charlie befriended many of the Eagles players. Charlie was club champion a few times and bagged a half dozen holes-in-one in his career. Amateur golf was big news then and Charlie's picture was always in the paper for winning this tourney or that.

Why he is taking me to the Championship game?

But the obvious question was why would Uncle Charlie take me? Why not his wife? His own kids? Simple, they all told him he was nuts and they weren't going any place in this monster blizzard. "Hey, why not take Teddy?" one of them suggested and so I got the call.

Did I want to go? Of course. I'm a kid. I'm also a sports nut – since birth, I assume. It was a football game, why wouldn't I want to go. I had never been to one before. A little snow was no big deal to me.

So Mom bundled me up like a mummy in boots, leggings, sweaters, a big wooly hat and mittens. I then trudged up the street – we lived in the middle of the block - and they were two houses in off of Limekiln Pike (the street where Mom and Clare grew up).

Making the walk was a chore. I'd take a couple of steps and the snow would drive me back a couple. There was a small path up the center where a truck had driven by so I made my way out to it and plodded up to Uncle Charlie's. I was just eight. There was little danger of anything running me over; only idiots would venture out in a storm like this one. I qualified as an idiot, I suppose. Amazingly, my Mom opted to stand on our front porch and watch me, rather than actually accompany me. Mom was a lot smarter than I realized.

The Glenside Kid

When I arrived Charlie was out front brushing the snow off his monster-sized Oldsmobile. The chains were on, the motor was roaring, his defroster was defrosting and the coast was clear. We were ready to go.

I climbed in the front seat, my Uncle eyed me up and said, "You look like you are going to the Yukon or someplace." I laughed and blamed my Mom for dressing me like this. Charlie, a hunter, had one of those red plaid Elmer Fudd hats on, a thick plaid coat and heavy boots. He was an outdoorsman and this adventure clearly appealed to him.

The Olds was like a truck. It dug in and off we went. We encountered very little traffic. The car was warm as toast, the heater was chugging along just fine, thank you. I was as happy as could be. It was an adventure and I was going to love it.

It took us about an hour to get to 21st and Lehigh – the location of Shibe Park – in North Philly and, to my amazement, the closer we got the more traffic we encountered. I had been to the park, before, for baseball but never for a football game.

Due to the bad weather I think a lot of people took public transportation to the game because the Reading and Pennsylvania Railroads both had stations within walking distance of the ball park – and the trains always seemed to get through in those days, unlike today when mere flurries seem to shut them down. I guess the tracks didn't ice up in those days.

For a little history, the 1948 National Football League Championship game was the 16th NFL title game played. The NFL didn't have the wide fan following of today's pro game, in fact the Eagles were regularly outdrawn in the city by both Penn and Temple football games. The jury was still out on whether pro football would ever be viable and supplant the college game nationally.

The game was actually a rematch of the previous year's championship game between the Chicago Cardinals, champions of

The Glenside Kid

the Western Division and the Philadelphia Eagles, champions of the Eastern Division. As my aunt had pointed out to my uncle he could have stayed home and watched it on TV because it was the first NFL championship game to be televised. They had, as I recall, a Dumont television in their living room.

If you recall the early days of TV – rabbit ears and all - "snow" was a frequent problem, but in this case the snow was going to be real.

When we finally made out way in to the park – and got to our 50-yard-line seats (Charlie knew people) we noticed that both the grounds crew and the players from both teams were actually out on the field shoveling snow. Once they got the snow off the tarp that was covering the field, the players and the crew wrestled it in to a role and pushed it against the third base stands – not so far from where we were sitting. Can you imagine today's NFL millionaire players shoveling snow? No, neither can I.

Uncle Charlie had a flask – and it didn't contain coffee. My Mom sent me with a thermos and it did contain hot Ovaltine – which I loved then, still love to this day.

Bert Bell, the commissioner of the NFL and the man who put pro football on the map, had considered postponing the game but the players for both teams wanted to play. The attendance for the game was announced at 36,309 – I can't imagine there were that many crazy people in all of Philadelphia. Uncle Charlie and I accounted for two of that number. The stands were never actually full, I think a lot of the 36,309 bought tickets and then opted to stay home.

As far as games went – and to be honest we spent a fairly large portion of our time under the stands in the concourse trying to keep warm – it was pretty dull. And boy was it cold.

The Glenside Kid

Steve Van Buren scores the Eagles winning TD, and that's him on my autographed 1948 Leaf football card

The Eagles were dressed in their home white uniforms, making them vanish from time-to-time and the Cardinals had on red jerseys. The teams played to a scoreless duel for most of the game – you could hardly see the yard markers, the players were stiff and kind of looked like frozen zombies - and then early in the fourth quarter, after Chicago had fumbled deep in their own end of the field, the Eagles recovered the ball and that set up future Hall of Famer Steve Van Buren's five yard touchdown run at 1:05 in to the

The Glenside Kid

fourth quarter. Cliff Patton, a guard from the unlikely hometown of Clyde, Texas (I knew that from my football cards) kicked the extra point and that's all the scoring there was. We could have all gone home then, but there was still time to play so we stayed. Nothing else of any consequence happened, though. It just kept snowing and we kept getting colder.

As we drove back to Glenside Uncle Charlie and I talked about the game like we were old pals. He seemed as though he actually liked me. I was so happy – and so very cold. But by the time we hit our neighborhood I had thawed out, the heater in the Olds was remarkable and could have melted glaciers. When got back home he drove up Oak Road and actually made it a point to stop in front of my house and let me out. "Thanks for going with me," he said. I thanked him in return. It was one of the greatest days of my little boy life.

My best Christmas present in 1950 was an autograph book. Uncle Charlie got the 1950 Eagles to sign it. I still have it and look at the signatures and recall and wonderful time and the thoughtfulness of a tough guy who was also a pretty nice man.

The Eagles quarterback, Tommy Thompson, was a close friend of Uncle Charlie's and his is the first name on the list. Thompson, out of Tulsa, OK only had one eye – and yet was eclipsed only by the immortal Sammy Baugh as an NFL player in their era. I met Mr. Thompson one day when he was visiting at their house.

Also in the autograph book are Chuck Bednarik, Walt Stikel, Jack Myers, Norm Willey, Joe Muha, Al Wistert, Duke Maronic, Vic Sears, Cliff Patton, Frank Reagan, Bosh Pritchard, John Magee, Mario Gianelli, Alex Wojiehowicz, John Green, Steve Van Buren, Bucko Kilroy, Bill Hix and Neill Armstrong – a few of them Hall of Famers. Would I ever part with it? Not on your life.

Chapter XI - The twins almost lived in Glenside, too.

Brett and Colleen (plus the twins) reside in North Wales PA, but they came within a whisker of buying their first house, shortly after they were married, right across the street from my boyhood abode on Oak Road in Glenside. I was thrilled when they considered the home but, as a longtime local political columnist, understood why they didn't buy it.

For all the good things about Glenside in Cheltenham Township there are also some bad things. Among them onerous, really out of whack school taxes and much-too-high real estate taxes that bleed the middle classes like few municipalities around. By comparison, Abington is a tax oasis.

Glenside covers more than 1300 acres and is divided into two distinct parts and is governed by two townships: Abington and Cheltenham. It is located one mile north of the Philadelphia city limits and ten miles north of center city.

I grew up in the Cheltenham part of Glenside; the township dividing line was Mt. Carmel Avenue. Glenside kids from Abington did not always mix well with Glenside kids from Cheltenham – the exception being when we all attended the same church. In my case that would be Carmel Presbyterian at 100 Edge Hill Road, but it could have been St. Luke's RC Church, Glenside Methodist or others that served both townships..

Glenside's history dates back to William Penn, who deeded much of the land to families who owned them for many years. Many sections and streets adopted the early settler's names. Roger Tyson, who emigrated from Germany in 1685, set up lime-burning kilns in the area in Roslyn in 1718 thus creating the name "Limekiln Pike". It was that street on which my Roth grandparents resided and raised eight children. It was but a dirt road when they first moved there. When they settled in to their home it wasn't Glenside at all, but was known as Harmer Hill.

The Glenside Kid

Montgomery County was part of Philadelphia, the nation's capitol, until 1784. During the Revolutionary War, a pitched battle was fought at Edge Hill and Easton Roads (very near where I live today), in which more men were killed and wounded than in any other part of Montgomery County. As a kid I remember them digging up the bones of some Revolutionary war soldiers and then attending the ceremony – I went there on my bicycle - when they re-buried them on the site of the North Penn VFW Post 676. As a country we were more patriotic then.

Abington Station was Glenside's name at the time of the civil war with only six houses in the whole town. The "Glenside" name was created March 7, 1887(13 years after the Roth's settled there), with the establishment of the first post office. Easton Road was known as Plank Road, then extending from Mount Airy to Willow Grove.

At the dawn of the 20th century the Casa Conti Restaurant (now New Life Presbyterian Church) was known as the Weldon Hotel, a popular stage coach stop with a toll booth in operation on the opposite corner. Celebrities who were appearing at the Keswick Theatre nearby made the Weldon their favorite destination.

Trolleys began running about 1900 – and this mode of transportation also lead to the creation of Willow Grove Park. As a kid in the 50's I'd walk over to the Royal Avenue trolley stop (near where Bishop McDevitt High School is located today) and I spent many a summer afternoon riding the Thunderbolt and the Little Scenic. The trolley also sped me to Cheltenham Avenue – within walking distance of Temple Stadium if I turned right and the Lynne Lanes bowling alleys if I turned left.

The community's first bank, the Glenside National Bank was founded in 1909. The bank later changed its name to the Glenside Bank and Trust Company and is now the PNC Bank at Easton Rd. and Glenside Avenue. The Glenside Public Library Association organized the first library in 1928 and, after several moves – including a long stint in a large house during my childhood on

Easton Road just above Waverly – they built a new building in 1968 at Keswick Ave and Waverly Road.

Chapter XII - Glenside was a great "hometown"

Growing up in Glenside in the 1940's and 50's was about the best thing that could have happened to a kid. It was a great place to live. People liked each other, cared about them and interacted as if we were one big family. If Normal Rockwell had ever found it, he'd have painted it in to his Americana pictures. The old-timey July 4 Parade has been going for well over 100 years and to this day draws thousands of onlookers from near and far.

It was a place where no one ever locked their doors, you left your car keys in the ignition and in the summer, if you went on vacation, you left the windows open to keep the placed aired out. If we ever wanted to lock the house, we locked the back door. We never had a key for the front. It had been misplaced shortly after my parents moved there in 1941. In the morning when you came down to breakfast you found the milk bottles in your refrigerator where the milkman – who entered through the back door – had left them.

My Mom's family had deep roots in Glenside and most of them – and their kids, too – lived a good part of their lives there...or close by. Much of the Roth family is buried in Hillside Cemetery in Roslyn.

The boyhood home at 338 Oak Road

The Glenside Kid

I can still walk down Oak Road and tell you who lived in just about every house. They were, mostly, twins though there was a single house at both ends of the street – and on both sides of it. We had the only Oak tree on Oak Road – and it was there until 2009 when it was struck by lightening and took out pieces of three adjoining houses.

It was pretty much a white-collar neighborhood, with some blue collar types mixed in. Actually that was an apt description of most of Glenside. But weren't about status in those days. People took each other at face value.

My side of the street started with the Hager family at the Limekiln Pike end, then the Jordans, the Golds, the McKays, the Renningers, the Ewings, the Krahs, the Seeley's (pretty, but older than me daughter Bobbie), the Cliffs (pretty, younger than me, daughter Karen), the Hartings, our house, the Sculleys (their son Peter J. Sculley the third "lived in a tree like a bird, we'd sing), the Gays, the Whittingtons, the Tarlows, the McCafferty's, the Dierings and along the way the Kelley's (daughter Lurline was named after a Hawaiian cruise ship) and on the corner the Bamfords (daughter named Honey, who was one).

The other side started, again at Limekiln, with the Loves (granddaughter Phyllis, an early love interest of mine whose parents moved to Columbia SC thus pretty much ending any future thoughts either of us had), The Lavisi's, my Aunt Clare and Uncle Charlie, the Oberholtzers, the Haynes, the Kings, the Gruns (Ed Grun was mean, kind of like Mr. Wilson in "Dennis the Menace" and we were all scared of him), the Mahwinney's and the Wilsons, the Refsnyders, the Doughertys, the McClellans, the Gillums and all the way down to the Delzingaros and my mom's dear friend Aunt Lil Meyer. There were transient houses on both sides of the street where people seemed to come and go, and they were always the same ones. The regulars got there and stayed there.

Walter Wilson, directly across the street from us, was the travel editor of the *Philadelphia Evening Bulletin* and encouraged

The Glenside Kid

my interest in journalism. Dick Refsnyder was one of the Glenside's greatest semi-pro baseball players (in the 30's when semi pro was almost as good as the big leagues). Old-timers would tell you that Dick and Walt Hawkins, another local baseball hero, were good enough to play in the majors. Dick, who later in life managed the local semi pro team, also kept me supplied with baseballs and bats.

Bob Tarlow was a Cheltenham cop (and father of 11 kids) and the first one on the scene when my step father died of a massive heart attack, at home, after returning from a New Year's eve get together with friends in 1961. Dave Gillum, a boyhood friend, became a well respected physician in Williamsport, PA. Ken Renninger was a prominent Glenside realtor (his daughter Carol, a lifelong friend), Dr. Edward Krah was a longtime school principal in the Abington school system and Dr. Onslow B. Hager was a well known scientist.

The street had many interesting people in that one little block. Diversity? We had it, at least as it was in those days. We had everything but Asians and African Americans on our street, but I got to know and be good friends several African Americans at my elementary school. Before my teen years were over I discovered Jews as they moved in to a new development in Glenside right up the street from me – and in close proximity to the new Glenside School.

Actually my first real encounter with Jewish kids came on the playground of the new Glenside School. I was a teenager and shooting baskets with my friend Bill Robinson. We thought we were pretty hot stuff. Along came two kids, twin brothers obviously, who introduced themselves as Steve and Marty Rosen. They said they were new to the neighborhood. Obviously they lived in the new houses that were built behind the school. They asked if they could play. We said, sure, why not. And so we decided on a two-on-two contest. Bill was tall, I was older – we got smoked. The Rosen twins were good. No, check that. They were the best kid basketball players we ever saw. Later they both went on to outstanding hoops achievements at Cheltenham High and in college.

Negroes or colored people, as they were called in those days, lived in the Edge Hill or North Hills sections of Glenside and, as my Mom often pointed out, had been there since the Civil War. Richie Cottom was my first black friend, Tommy Lampkin came a year or two later. I met Richie in kindergarten, Tommy in third grade as I recall. They were kids, just like us, only a different color. There were also a lot of Italians in North Hills and they, too, had been a part of Glenside for decades. The Italian kids out of North Hills tended to be the "tough" guys at school. Our street, itself, tilted to the Anglo Saxon persuasion but more than a few Catholic and Italian families were also part of the mix.

Glenside Elementary School was at the intersection of Easton Road and Springhouse Lane. My mom and her siblings all went there – and I went there too. The playground was cinders on one side, macadam on the other and a creek ran by the side of the property. There was a Texaco Station directly opposite the school and, once, the owner gave free fire hats to about 50 kids who then all wore them to class. The principal, Miss Esther Taggart, went nuts and made us all return them. Fast talker that I was, I convinced Miss Taggart that my fire hat predated the Texaco station give away and she bought it. I kept mine.

Across Easton Road from the school was a large open field where I spent countless hours of my youth playing baseball and football. There was a sign posted there in memory of my father. It read "No Golf". Dad had a penchant for going down there and hitting golf balls, sometimes in to the yards of neighbors. It pissed them off enough to complain to the township about it. Dad figured, "hey it's an open lot, and it was cheaper than going down to golfing legend Skee Reigel's driving range in Cedarbrook."

The Glenside Kid

Glenside Elementary – My mother went there, so did I

Below the school, toward downtown Glenside, was a string of gas stations along Easton Road. My Mom's childhood friend Gene "Fee Cent" Riley owned the Esso station, but she didn't go there – or to the Mobilgas Station next door, or even the Sinclair. Nope her filling station of choice was the Richfield station owned by Al Cors at the corner of Easton and Waverly Roads. Al had a "kid" named Shorty Zimmerman working for him and mom liked them both. They wore gray uniforms, a military style cap, a black bow tie and washed your windshield, checked your oil, put air in your tires and sold you gas for around 25-cents-a-gallon.

The shopping center boasted two super markets – the Acme on the corner of Glenside Avenue and Easton Road and the A&P across the street in the middle of the block. My mom did her shopping at the Acme but bought all her meats from Harry Hankin's butcher shop on Glenside Avenue. Harry had been the butcher at the Acme and then went out on his own. My Mom and step father became social friends with the Hankins as well. Harry's shop was opposite Rizzo's Pizzeria – as kids we called it "The Pits" and it is where I first learned to love tomato pies and, later, pizza. Rizzo's was also a place where I'd stop on the way home from junior high football practice, buy a hoagie for 35-cents, eat it there, and then be home in time for dinner.

The Glenside Kid

Ronnie's 5&10 loomed large on Easton Road with its' black façade and large chrome letters. It was owned by the Lodge family and named for their son. But my favorite spot was Lew's Smoke Shop, right next to the 5&10. The owner was Lew Waxman, also a friend of our family. I bought all my baseball magazines and comic books in there – not to mention most of my candy. He sold a neat dark chocolate candy bar called a "Sportsman's Bracer". I never saw them anywhere else. There was also Jerry Gassel's men's clothing store, a couple of bars and a place that sold luggage. Glenside Hardware was on Easton Road opposite another bank – and it's still there today. My guess is they last remodeled it when I was ten, but that's what makes the place so cool to this day. If you can't find it in there, it doesn't exist.

I bought a lot of my baseball cards at the White Pharmacy, next to the Girard Trust Corn Exchange Bank, or at Koenig's drug store which was under the railroad bridge and up a block. A snapshot in my mind takes me back to 1952 when I went in to White's, bought my first pack of Bowman baseball cards, and then sat outside on the curb opening the packs. The first card I pulled was Willard Ramsdell. Why do I remember that? I have no idea.

Below Koenig's, on the opposite side of the bridge was Kirkland Printing. On the second floor, the printer, was a music studio where I went to take guitar lessons. It was called, grandly, "The Academy of Theatre Arts". Mom paid good money and I hated every moment of it and learned only to play "Lady of Spain" and that not very well. I had a Gene Autry guitar, but Gene never knew how bad I played it. Paul Kaiser and Paul Kariga were the teachers and I was one challenge they failed to overcome.

Sometimes, on my red Firestone bike, I'd ride to Keswick Avenue and visit either Tompkin's Corner or Sheehan's variety store where they, occasionally, got their baseball cards before the two drug stores. I remember that Tompkin's had the 1953 Topps baseball cards before anyone else. We'd troll the stores looking for the always exciting "new series" of card. I was familiar with that area of Keswick Avenue because the War Memorial Park (now

The Glenside Kid

Renninger Park) where I played baseball for the Glenside Midgets was there – and so was the Glenside swimming pool. I virtually lived at both during the summer.

Up the road from there, just above Mt. Carmel Avenue, was a non descript garage that was, to us paper boys, "The branch". It was where we went daily – and Sunday – to get our newspapers to deliver. I was a paper boy who delivered *The Bulletin* and the money I made financed my baseball card hobby and the rest of my social life such as it was.

The Fanelli Brothers barbershop was at Keswick and Mt. Carmel and there was a deli across the street where older looking teens could usually score a six-pack of cheap beer. The Glenside Theatre was next to the deli.

There was Gunn's Bakery at the far corner of Easton and Mt. Carmel Avenues - near St. Luke's Roman Catholic Church - and my mom often got our sticky buns there. Our family doctor, Karl Mayer, had his office at 355 N. Easton Rd. It was a doctor's office where I have spent considerable time in my life. Karl's nephew Donald took over the practice and then, Michael Lyons, who is still there kept the ball rolling. All three have been our family physicians.

Up the road a bit further, past Keswick Avenue and Gerhard's appliances, was the fabulous Casa Conti restaurant where we ate many a Sunday dinner on the way home from Carmel Presbyterian Church. One hallmark of the restaurant was that all the waitresses were "seasoned". They had been there a long time and they knew their business. I attended countless Scouts banquets, sports banquets and my sister, Pat, had her wedding reception there. Something went wrong at the reception and I can still recall seeing my sister, white gown and all, reaming out Mrs. Conti.

Not exactly Glenside, but still in our environs, right across the street from Willow Grove Park was the first hamburger drive-in that I was ever aware of. It was called Burger Chef and my Mom and I would sometimes treat ourselves to a 19-cent burger on the

The Glenside Kid

way home from church if we didn't go to Conti's. You ate your burger in the car, of course. Luigi's steak house was also nearby, but we stayed away from it. The story was that they served horsemeat – some opined that it was really Kangaroo meat. Which I doubt, but when the word gets out, it's kind of hard to overcome it.

Politically Glenside, and all of Montgomery County, was Republican. Democrats offered token opposition in local and county elections but had no chance of being elected – except as a mandated minority.

Mom was a Republican committee woman and always worked the polls. When Dwight D. Eisenhower ran for president she was constantly bedecked in "I like Ike" buttons, jewelry and, even, an Ike hat. As her kid, I had more Ike buttons than most – and found that I could trade them to kids at school for other things – like baseball cards, for instance.

That's Harry Renninger, right, handing me a football for the ceremonial opening of the 1960 season in Glenside

I don't know whether Harry Renninger was really my "Godfather" or not, but Mom called him that. Harry was, first, a township commissioner and, later, a county commissioner. The War Memorial Park in Glenside was renamed in his honor. Harry had "juice". An example was when Chuck Danihel and I formed the Glenside Gorillas midget football team we needed a place for our

The Glenside Kid

home games. We called on Harry and, presto, goal posts were erected at the War Memorial Field, bleachers arrived and the township crew lined the field for us for each home game. That's power.

Chapter XIII – Negotiate, but don't back down

The babies were born, healthy and happy, life is good. But it goes on regardless. We all face challenges and how we deal with them usually shapes the way we turn out.

I never told my kids to back down from a fight – if it was inevitable – but before doing battle I told them to always try to negotiate a settlement. Sometimes they did, sometimes they didn't.

The Philadelphia suburbs in the 1940's and 50's were more like living in the country. Lots of open space, generally quiet, few confrontations. Today Glenside, Abington, Jenkintown, Willow Grove are, for some reason, more like Mt. Airy and Germantown were when I was a kid – lots of people, lots of noise, lots of cars, stores everywhere. The urban sprawl has consumed the near suburbs.

As kids we felt safe and confrontations were few and far between– and when they happened it was more likely than not an argument about sports and whether a ball was hit fair or foul.

But every paradise has a problem far beyond sports every so often – and I had mine. The problem was a kid in our school – same grade as me, and a self-styled tough guy.

You hear about bullying and the problems that go along with it. The intimidation, the abuse and it isn't good. Adults try to deal with it, the President even wants to legislate it, but one day as a small boy I dealt with the problem head on. It was the only avenue left to me.

A friend asked me the other day how I learned to fight? Simple, I said, I learned from the cowboy movies I saw. It isn't that complicated, really.

Chapter XIV - Billy Buck and I do battle

Glenside Elementary School was a special place for me. It was very near to my home but, beyond that, it was a source for information. And I've always enjoyed learning things.

It was in first grade when I learned what my name was. How's that again? You got to first grade and didn't know your own name? Six years without a name?

Well, as you may recall, my Dad, named Henry, didn't want me to be named Henry because he didn't like the name. My Mom wanted me named for Dad; he wanted me named for his hero Theodore Roosevelt. So when Dr. George Gallen delivered me at the Jewish Hospital in Philadelphia the birth certificate read "Henry Roth Taylor" and my father started calling me "Teddy". The nickname stuck, everyone called me Teddy.

I grew up Teddy. I was Teddy in kindergarten and Miss Sudlow had no problems with that. But when I got to first grade and on the very first day of school I ended up in the Principal's office because when the teacher called out the role no one answered to "Henry Taylor" and as I sat there I realized that no one had called my name. The teacher was chagrined and sent me up the hall to the principal.

A phone call from the principal, Miss Esther Taggart, to my mother cleared up the mystery and I returned to class and resumed being known as "Teddy" at school.

I lived so close to school that I went home for lunch every day. I'd sail up the street and walk through the back door just as radio announcer Ted Collins was saying, "its high noon in New York and time for Kate Smith" and then I'd eat my lunch – usually a bowl of soup, often tomato - as Ted and Kate talked about stuff and she sang an occasional song. Mom liked Kate Smith and she also had her string of soap operas lined up to listen to as she performed her weekly chores. There was "wash day", "ironing day", "cleaning day", shopping day and, on Fridays, she met with other Oak Road ladies and had a regular "Tea party". It's the way it was. No one ever questioned that. Tuesday night was bridge club and that was life in the 50's.

I loved school and, frankly, was pretty good at it. My early report cards suggested I was a good student, very interested and willing to learn. The teachers seemed to like me. I also was involved in stuff, plays, safety patrol, you name it and was hardly ever absent for fear I'd miss something.

Billy, the school bully

The school had a bully. His name was Billy Arbuckle (the kids feared him as "Billy Buck" – and that sounded "tough") and he terrorized us all. His last name started with an A and mine with a T so we seldom were ever in the same homeroom. He had his legion of hangers on, the tough kids, the ones that my Dad would tell me "be nice to them, one day they'll be collecting your trash". And so I tried to avoid them.

The problem with that idea was that Billy was hard to avoid. He was like a pesky gnat, always around. We'd go out on the cinder laden playground for recess every morning at 10.30 AM. It was then that Billy would intimidate kids, shake them down for their lunch money and otherwise make life for his victim du jour unbearable. At one time or another he terrorized all of my friends.

One day he made a mistake. It was the spring of 1949, I was in third grade and he picked on me once too often. Billy didn't suspect that it was a mistake at the time and, really, neither did I. Like most self-styled toughs Billy didn't need a real reason to pick on you. This day he decided that he didn't like the cowboy shirt and bandana that I was wearing. He started making fun of me for liking cowboys and snatched the bandana from around my neck – my Roy Rogers official neckerchief holder tumbling to the playground - and he was laughing like a hyena. Arbuckle was feeling full of himself,

The Glenside Kid

he was ready to terrorize yet another kid, when my mind short-circuited and I blew a fuse.

The very outfit I was wearing when Billy and I went to war, that's Roy Rogers and Trigger on my pocket

I screamed unintelligible things at him, then I charged at him, knocking him to the cinders. He was stunned and speechless. I sat on top of Billy and started to beat the crap of him. I was, as Jean Shepherd once wrote, "speaking in tongues". (If you saw Ralphie do it to a bully in the popular movie *A Christmas Story* written by Shepherd, you saw me, too.) It was almost like I was having an out of body experience. Teddy Taylor doesn't beat people up. I had no idea who this kid was who was throttling Billy, but he sure was something.

None of bully's friends wanted any part of me. They steered clear, a few recused themselves to a far corner of the playground. In truth Billy and I were about the same size, but he just seemed bigger. He always dressed in tough guy outfits – flannel shirt, blue jeans, and scuffed shoes. He certainly was nastier, a kid that was a perpetual pain in the rear.

The Glenside Kid

My friends, who comprised the legions of Billy's previous victims, were cheering me on. And then the bell rang to return to class. Arbuckle was literally saved by the bell. I was a mess, but Billy was even worse off. My knuckles were bleeding, my shirt was torn, I had ripped out the knee of my pants but he looked like he was hit by a train. Billy had a bloody nose, his shirt was torn off – the buttons all popped, it was now just a shredded rag – and he was on the verge of a black eye. Which a day later was a real beauty.

I knew I couldn't go back in to school looking like I did so I simply ran home. Billy did go back in to the school and his teacher, Miss Waughtel, looked at him in horror. "What happened she asked?" and he managed to tell her, despite his bawling, "Teddy Taylor beat me up". She asked him where I was. He said he didn't know. My friends chimed in and explained that Billy, as usual, had started things but, this time, he didn't get to finish them.

Meanwhile I went home and I walked in the back door of our house. My Mom was downstairs doing the wash. I looked a wreck when I climbed down the cellar steps and when she saw me she gasped. "What happened?" She wanted to know and I told her. "Billy Arbuckle picked on me once too often," I blubbered. I then added, "So I beat the daylights out of him". Which I, in fact, had.

Mom cleaned me up, washed out the cinders from my knees and bandaged my scrapes. She gave me a new shirt and pants and walked me back to school. Miss Waughtel, and the rest of the faculty, breathed a sigh of relief when I came in. (Later she told my mother that she, first, thought Billy might have killed me. Everyone knew that he was a bully and I never understood why they let him get away with it.)

Within minutes we were all in Miss Taggart's office – except Billy's parents, both of whom worked and neither of whom wanted anything to do with him anyway. The principal gave us a lecture on "getting along with one another". That was it, nothing else happened. Today we'd have both been expelled...or worse.

The Glenside Kid

Billy's days as the school bully were over. Kids that he had picked on before began picking on him. As a result he actually got to be a pretty decent kid, self preservation I suppose. In fact we kind of became friends; at least we co-existed without any more violence. But it was something that needed doing and I had done it. Eventually Billy moved away and was never heard from again.

Life as it was at Glenside School

We didn't have a student council or anything at Glenside Elementary, but what we did have was a Safety Patrol – and all the good kids got to be "Safeties". With it came this nifty white belt (looking somewhat like the Sam Brown belts worn by the police) and a badge that identified you as a member of the "Keystone Safety patrol". As such you got to help kids across the street and make sure they were all inside when the bell rang. At the end of the day the safety patrol members got to bring the flag down outside the main entrance.

Each year the safety patrol members had an outing to the ballpark and, in 1951, we went to an A's-Yankees game and I got to see the great Joe DiMaggio play. It was the only time I ever saw him in uniform.

You got elected to the safety patrol from your homeroom and when you hit fifth grade you could run for lieutenant and, in sixth grade, captain. Pretty cool stuff, really.

I ran twice and was elected once. I got to be lieutenant in fifth grade but lost to my friend Larry Strange for captain in sixth grade. I still remember my campaign slogan "You'll Rocket Ahead if you vote for Ted". Not enough of my friends rocketed.

I did a clean student council sweep in junior high and high school getting elected as my homeroom rep for six straight years. I could never figured out if that was due to my charm and popularity or that no one else wanted the job. In those six years, though, I

The Glenside Kid

never aspired to a higher administrative school-wide elected office on student council. There were just too many other things to do.

Rats as big as cats..and Cub Scouts too

Glenside School was old; it had cloak rooms behind the blackboard. One day a new teacher, Miss Helen Applegate, looking like a school teacher did in those days – stern, conservative clothing, prim hair style - showed up to take over our fifth grade class.

She was teaching us something, her back to the class, writing on the blackboard when all of a sudden she left out a blood curdling shriek that would have awakened the dead. And as she yelled bloody murder she ran out the door of the classroom - leaving about 25 of us totally bewildered.

And then, around the corner from the cloak room, came a cute gray kitty cat.

Minutes later Miss Applegate came back with the janitor, Mr. Folk, and was amazed to see us all playing with the cat. She was totally embarrassed, she said, and then told us that when she first arrived at the school someone had warned her that the creek that ran by the school was populated with "rats as big as cats" and when the gray head peeped around the corner her mind said "rat" not "cat".

Sometime later someone put an actual rat (albeit quite dead) in her desk drawer. It was the same drawer where all the water pistols, sling shots and other kiddie ammunition that she had confiscated was kept. She found no humor at all in the dead rat, but handled it much better than before. I thought it was inspired and wished I had thought of it.

Glenside School was also home to our Cub Pack 38 meetings. The Cub master was Henry Parks – father of my friend and classmate Hank Parks. A woman named Polly Clark was our den mother. I earned all the badges, little silver and gold arrow

The Glenside Kid

patches plus the Wolf, Bear, Lion and even Webelos awards. I learned how to carve owls out of Fels Naphtha soap among other life skills. It was a lot of fun and most of my friends were Cubs. We once went to the Boy Scout camp, Delmont, and it rained the whole time. I've never been much of an outdoorsman. Kids don't do any of that Scout stuff as much any more and I think they're missing something.

Our official uniform was made up of a blue shirt, blue pants, yellow bandana, and blue cap. You needed the complete uniform or you got demerits. Today kids wear the shirt, never matching pants, and I don't see the cap much either. We were neat, crisp, and almost military. Not so today. Heck I even wore a Cub knife on my belt which would, as a lethal weapon, get you expelled from school in this era of zero tolerance. It never occurred to us to actually stab someone with our scout knives.

I was at a den meeting; it was 1951, when my Mother called to ask Mrs. Clark to send me home. She told her that "someone important" was there and they wanted to see me. It was four blocks from Clarks to our house, but I covered it in record time, wondering who this 'someone" might be.

As I came through the door I realized that the 'someone" was, instead, a "something". Mom had, somehow, come up with the money and there, resplendent in our living room was a 12-inch Philco TV. Life was good; no forget that, it was wonderful. I felt so many emotions – happy, giddy, shocked, elated, and dumfounded – and it was one of my young life's happiest days.

No more long walks to the neighbors to watch TV. The Taylor's (both of us, really) now were TV owners and life was good. I was in for daily and weekly doses of my favorite shows - *Howdy Doody, Willie the Worm, Frontier Playhouse, Mr. I Imagination, You are there, Kukla Fran and Ollie, Cecil the Seasick Sea Serpent, Yukon King, Your Hit Parade* and, of course, *Roy Rogers, Gene Autry* and *The Cisco Kid*.

Chapter XV – All the nuts are not in the jar

One day on the way home from visiting the twins we pulled the Taurus in to the driveway of our house and my wife said, "Look at that guy over there, I think there's something wrong with him."

And I looked – and there was. The guy was clearly not playing with the same number of cards in his deck as you and I. He was tall, about 6'2, slim, wearing a long black coat and had on a head band. I had no idea who he was. The guy was running up the opposite side of the street yelling "Lila where are you?" And I was kind of afraid he was going to ask me, because I didn't know..

When he couldn't find Lila he started yelling for "Michael, where are you?" and I said to Cindy that if Michael and Lila have any sense they'll steer clear of this guy too. We did.

I never saw him after that, and hope I never do. But we have to accept that the world abounds with characters – some would call them nut jobs. Whatever they are called they are also part of the landscape and little Brett and Lily will, no doubt, encounter their share of them along the way.

As my friend, Dr. Elaine Green, Dean of continuing and professional studies at Chestnut Hill College gets right to the point and is fond of saying, "All the nuts are not in the jar."

Chapter XVI – Glenside had its' share of characters

My childhood chums and I weren't the only characters in our old neighborhood. No, there were others and among the most memorable were "Mr. Flynn" and a man we knew only as "Rum and Coke".

Mr. Flynn, I have no idea what his first name was (I just assumed it was "Mister", what does a kid know?), had been the chauffeur of the "Sugar King", the master of the William Welsh Harrison family that called the Grey Towers castle at what is now Arcadia University, home.

Grey Towers Castle
The Harrison Family Home
Church & Limekiln Pike, Glenside
Circa 1900

When the Harrison's divorced and their fabulous estate was sold to the college (then it was Beaver, all girls) Mr. Flynn moved to a small house on Limekiln Pike – or perhaps he always lived there, I don't really know - and, as my Mom told me, he lived on a modest pension. One thing he did retain was the Harrison's Packard, which he kept in gem mint condition and, daily, drove down our street on his way to someplace.

Perhaps he really didn't have a destination at all because he drove no more than 15 MPH – we ran along side the car many days.

We could have beaten it, he was going so slowly. He wore immaculate clothing, a chauffeurs hat and was always fixated on the road. He clearly loved his Master's car and he treated it as if it were a treasured relic. Today it would be priceless.

And then there was old "Rum and Coke".

He was a strong candidate for being the town drunk, and he boarded at Dougherty's house across the street from ours. I don't really know if he was even old. But he looked old. Booze ages you. His real name? No one ever said, maybe nobody knew.

Now I can't testify that the man tippled but the story was that if you hit on "Rum and Coke" at precisely the right time you'd probably come out of the experience a good, solid twenty-five cents richer. I always steered clear of him. He had an aura, perhaps better described as an essence, about him and he always wore a big coat with a bulge in one pocket.

We figured that's where he kept the rum, if not the Coke.

He was a strange, if harmless, man. And then, one day, he was gone. We never knew if he died or just moved on to board elsewhere.

Richard's fiery experience

And, while recalling strange things, I still remember my friend Richard Cliff's fiery downfall and it all had to do with our collection of old Christmas trees. Why we collected old used Christmas trees I'll never know, but after every Christmas we did and then, for some reason, we piled them in the woods across from our homes.

I was seven, Richard was eight. He almost never saw nine.

One day we were playing cowboys and Indians in the woods – right after returning home from a Roy Rogers double-feature – and

The Glenside Kid

we decided that we should have a campfire to sit around, like the real cowboys did. As I recall, the plotline of our adventure du jour called for such a campfire, perhaps to keep the Indians at bay.

It was probably three or four o'clock in the afternoon and a campfire wasn't really needed but, hey, cowboys want what they want when they want it.

Richard had access to the kitchen cabinet at his house, the place where his Mom kept the matches, and so, after failing to ignite our campfire by rubbing sticks together (like the real cowboys always seemed to do with little effort), Richard went home and got the matches. As an aside, they also used magnifying glasses to light fires, too. I could never make that happen either.

Well we lit the fire with the matches and it was really a good one. In fact it was a little too good and we began to have visions of the woods catching fire. In fact almost each year of my boyhood some kid or another set the woods on fire. This looked like it was going to be our year, our turn.

Richard was a year older, hence one would assume brighter, and had this great idea. "Quick, hand me something green, that'll smother the fire" he said. And I did. That sentence almost turned out to be Richard's last words. A pile of old discarded Christmas trees was laying near by and they looked green to me...so I grabbed one and tossed it to him.

What happened next was and is etched in my memory like scenes from a horror movie.

I heard this "whoosh" noise and, almost like magic, Richard didn't have any more eyebrows, his hair was strangely sizzling and, overall, he was kind of a sooty color. He also had this real dopey look on his face. He seemed both amazed and stunned at the same time.

What had transpired, of course, was that the four-month-old Christmas tree that I had tossed his way may have looked green but it was as dry as a bone and it ignited as if it were a can of gasoline.

I had not only succeeded in setting Richard on fire but now the entire woods was ablaze. We ran for it and somebody saw the smoke and called the fire company…again. And the firemen, including my Uncle Dick, put the fire out and averted a calamity. Richard looked kind of funny until his eyebrows and hair grew back in, but no one held that against me. It was a ritual associated with growing up, that, if you survive it, makes for a nifty memory.

Frogs, tadpoles and other critters

In those same woods, when kids weren't setting them on fire, there were lots of critters. A summer day wouldn't go by when we didn't frequent the woods.

Catching frogs was big among us guys and it used to be a hoot to catch tadpoles and watch them grow up and become frogs. It was as close to an interest in biology as I'd ever muster.

Garter snakes were a nuisance. I liked to catch frogs and turtles and that sort of wildlife but those stupid garter snakes used to keep popping up and getting in the way. What good is a snake? All they did was slither and scare the bee jabbers out of little girls. Though, I must admit, there was an appealing quality to hearing girls scream when you confronted them with a little wiggly snake. We always heard tell of nasty snakes in our woods, like water moccasins or rattlesnakes, but never remember confronting one.

Back then if all you could catch was a cruddy old garter snake all your buddies looked down on you as a failure to the great fraternity of budding naturalists. I even remembered reading a book when I was in fifth grade that my idol and namesake, Teddy Roosevelt, used to go around rounding up frogs, turtles and other wildlife creatures as a boy. And that made perfect sense to me. Boys and creatures were a natural combination.

The Glenside Kid

Box turtles were also rather plentiful back in the days of my reckless boyhood, but I found out recently that you can't even buy one now if you wanted one. I wonder why? I know there are plenty of them at a golf course I frequent. I think they might be snappers and I never get very close to them to know for sure.

In the woods we'd also encounter deer from time-to-time. And there is nothing as thrilling for a little kid as to be startled senseless by a huge deer springing out in front of you. In hindsight it was very cool – and it's why, though I went deer hunting twice as an adult, I could never shoot one. I always figured it would be more sporting if the deer also had a gun and since that wasn't going to happen it seemed to be to be a colossal mis-match.

Chapter XVII - Getting a glove and a cap for Brett II

I was pretty pumped when I learned early on that one of the twins was going to be a boy. After all he was preceded by four girls – and was bringing another one with him. I dearly love my granddaughters, but a grandson would be nice, too, I reasoned.

"When little Brett arrives we need to get him a Phillies hat and a glove," I told Cindy. She suggested that, since father Brett was a big Flyer's fan, perhaps a hockey jersey would be more appropriate. In fact on one of our first visits to see the twins after they got home the four of them – Mom, Dad and the kiddies - were all attired in Flyers shirts.

"Nonsense", I said, "I'm the Grandfather and baseball is my sport. He'll get baseball stuff; let his father buy him hockey gear."

Baseball was always my number one sport. The other things – football and basketball (there was no ice hockey in our area when I was a kid) – were what you did between baseball seasons.

I would scour the newspapers daily, during the off season, for any trace of information about baseball I'd tune to Jim Leaming each day to find out what he knew on WIP at 6.45 PM. He always reminded me that "A winner never quits and a quitter never wins". My annual Christmas presents always included a copy of "The Sporting News", the Baseball Bible published in St. Louis. From that paper I'd clip pictures of baseball players for whom there were no actual cards, paste them on cardboard cut to the size of a bubblegum card and pack them in with the real cards to make a complete team for the various baseball card games we would cook up as kids.

I collected baseball cards since 1948 – and still do. My first cards were purchased in 1948, supplemented by a playing card sized issue of the year before from Bond Bread. Later in life I actually worked for one of the nation's largest baseball card producers – Fleer – and in the mid-70's created the largest baseball

The Glenside Kid

card hobby show – "The Philly Show" – in America. I also designed more than a few baseball card sets of my own.

Once, when I felt the need for a baseball uniform, I went in to Philly on the train, stopped at Pearson's sporting goods store, and bought a very spiffy one for myself. The downside of this purchase was that I was now fresh out of money to get my Mom a "Mother's Day" present. I solved the dilemma by giving her the baseball uniform – which she, in turn, gave back to me. She never allowed me to forget, however, the time I gave her a baseball uniform for Mother's Day.

I played and coached college baseball and have gone to countless major and minor league baseball games in my lifetime. Quite simply it is the sport I love.

When I was a young boy the Philadelphia Athletics were my favorite team – because they were my father's favorite team. That's the way it was in Philadelphia. As I boy I met Connie Mack one day – and later in life got to know his daughter, a few of his grandchildren and was fortunate enough to be the founding president of the Philadelphia Athletics Historical Society.

The Glenside Kid

Chapter XVIII - Connie Mack and Me

It's July, 1949, just a month after my father died, and my Uncle calls and says he's taking me to a baseball game at Shibe Park. My Mom gets me ready, he picks me up and off we go. I was still eight and Uncle Ernie (he was married to my Dad's sister Florence) was taking me to see the A's play the White Sox.

He picked me up in his Ford and we drove out of Glenside, we passed Beaver College, went down through Mt. Airy, past Nanny Taylor's house on Mt. Pleasant Avenue, down the Lincoln Drive – drove past Connie Mack's house, actually - and over Wissahickon Avenue to the ball park.

We parked the car on the street there in North Philadelphia, a blue collar working class neighborhood, and walked down Lehigh Avenue to where it intersected with 21st Street, right across the street from Dobbins Tech High School. We went in through the main gate and down a long corridor toward the interior of the ball park.

Connie Mack in 1949 flanked by coaches Earle Mack, Earl Brucker Sr., Al Simmons and Jimmie Dykes

Instead of going to our seats, though, my Uncle took me down a flight of stairs and right to the A's locker room in the bowels of the ball yard. Standing right outside the door was a very tall, very

The Glenside Kid

old looking, man in a fitted gray suit. The elderly man who was introduced as to me "Mr. Mack" by my Uncle Ernie was, of course Connie Mack.

"What do you want to be when you grow up?" the elderly man in the gray suit asked me and I told him, "I want to be a newspaperman or a teacher some day". Little did I know that I'd actually do both.

Now I had been to Shibe Park before. I went with my father in the mid-to-late 40's. Dad worked nearby at DeLong Hook & Eye Co., 20th & Clearfield Streets and would go in to the office on some Saturdays, do a little work and then would take me to a day game. My memory of the games is vague, but not the image of the pristine green grass, the rich brown infield dirt, the green painted ballpark itself and this wonderful smell of hot dogs and peanuts and cracker jacks, all blending together.

The ball park was impressive to a little kid. The rounded office tower by the main entrance – that housed Mr. Mack's office – stood like a beacon to baseball fans all over the city. Yes, the Phillies played here too (because their rickety old park down the street – at Broad and Lehigh – had literally fallen apart), but it was the A's yard and, somehow, that gave them an edge.

Mr. Mack was surprised by my answer. "Don't you want to be a ball player?" he asked. And, of course, I did. Knowing what I know now, about how he would sign guys off the sandlots, I should have told him, "Yes, Mr. Mack, I do want to be a ball player." Maybe he'd have offered a contract. I did tell him that being a ball player would be a most welcome occupation.

And I think that was the day I actually fell in love with baseball. Up to then my life was pretty much cowboys. As you know, I was a Roy Rogers disciple. Others liked Gene Autry better, but Roy was my guy and, for some reason, you couldn't really be a fan of both. Like in Philly where Republicans gravitated to the A's and Democrats liked the Phillies. My late Dad had been a friend of

Bernard Samuel, the last Republican Mayor of the city, and one Thanksgiving we watched the Thanksgiving Day parade from Mayor Samuel's office. Didn't every kid? Who thought it was something special. It never dawned on me.

And as we stood there talking to Mr. Mack the players starting filing out of the locker room and heading up the ramp to the dugout. They were an impressive crew, carrying their gloves, their other equipment (catcher Mike Guerra had his shin guards tucked under his arms) and a few carried bats.

Their uniforms were quite plain and yet they were elegant and, to me, majestic. A simple "A" on the left breast, a block number on the back. A simple blue piping on the jersey. They wore a blue cap with a matching white "A", white pants with a blue stripe down the side and blue socks. Simple but that was the way the A's looked then – and should always look.

Hank Majeski – both Hank and me are really named Henry

"Hey Ernie," said Hank Majeski, the third baseman who was batting .309 at the time and would go 1-for-4 in this game. My Uncle smiled and called him over. "Henry, meet Henry," he said. And then told Majeski that though I went by the name of Ted, my real name was Henry. Majeski smiled and said, "I get it, I'm not

The Glenside Kid

fond of being called Henry either." (They also called him "Heeney" which I think is even worse than Henry.) Immediately Hank Majeski became my favorite player.

Next I met Ferris Fain who also, for some reason, seemed to know my Uncle too. In fact Ernie called him "Burr" (short for his nickname "Burrhead", due to his short hair cut). Anyway Fain swaggered over and was introduced to me as well. Was this cool or what? Fain was only batting .246 at the time of the game but would go on to be the American League batting champion in both 1951 and 1952. Fain appeared to be a rough neck – and so was Uncle Ernie – I suspected they had shared a few draught beers together over the years. I later learned that, despite his considerable talents, Fain drove Mr. Mack crazy with his post game exploits.

A few seasons later I became the Glenside Midgets' first baseman and tried to play with the same reckless abandon at the position that made Fain famous. I had this cool "Trapper's mitt" and one day I charged down the line, ala Fain, expecting a bunt and the kid swung away and hit a line drive that was heading straight for my noggin before I dove out of the way. I made a note to tell Fain, one day, that he almost got me killed. And in the late 1990's at a Philadelphia A's reunion I did tell him and he thought it was quite funny.

I recall Ernie saying hello to Al Simmons, Eddie Joost, Lou Brissie who limped (from a war injury I later learned) and Elmer Valo. Some others too. Simmons looked very old to me. Unc told me "he's a coach, but was once one of the best players in baseball." Imagine that. Maybe I'll write a book about him some day, I thought.

How did he know these people? Later I life I learned that he was also pals with James H. J. Tate, who became Mayor of Philadelphia and that he had grown up in the same Philly neighborhood where the Italian huckster, was a man they called Mr. Campanella and who had a mixed race kid named Roy who was quite the catcher. At one point in the early 40's Mr. Mack had tried to sign Mr. Campanella's boy – calling him a "swarthy Italian", but there was no mistaking his African American heritage and it took the Brooklyn Dodgers and the guts of Branch Rickey to get him to the majors.

We had box seats so we were quite near the dugout. Ernie told me to "watch the old man" as he directed players with his scorecard. I did. And he did. I was hooked. Unc explained that the guy wearing number 27 was Mr. Mack's son Earle and that since the old man didn't wear a uniform and the rules wouldn't allow non-uniformed personnel on the field during the game, Earle had a job and was the guy who went to the mound to remove failing pitchers. "He might even be manager one day," my Uncle said and then, reconsidered and added, "But I seriously doubt it from what I've heard about him." Ernie was "connected" to the A's in some way that I never found out. He died much too young at age 52 – I was 21 – so I never got around to asking.

This trip to the old ball yard was for a night game and was something I had never seen before. With their 11-4 win over Chicago White Sox the A's regained second place in the American League, a half game ahead of the Detroit Tigers. The game was played for just 6,560 fans – the club didn't draw very well, but neither did the Phillies. The Yankees, of course, were in first place 4-and-a-half game ahead of the locals. It was the 62nd game of the year.

Big lefty Alex Kellner pitched the whole game for the A's running his record to 10-3. Sam Chapman was 4-for-5 (with a homerun), Eddie Joost 3-for-5 and young second baseman Nelson Fox was 2-for-2 (replacing the injured Pete Suder) and fielded flawlessly. Fox, I recalled, didn't look very old – and he wasn't. The A's, for some reason, always treated Fox as a kid and with little respect. Once they dealt him to the White Sox – a year later – he became a future Hall of Famer. The rumors abounded that Mr. Mack was slipping and, in fact, suffered bouts of dementia. He seemed okay to me, though. But trading Fox for second rate catcher

The Glenside Kid

Joe Tipton was hardly the move that someone on top of things would have made.

I still have the program (and the clipping from the next day's Bulletin). I also have the yearbook – with Connie Mack's picture on the cover, but over the years I lost the actual ticket. My Uncle also bought me a pennant, a copy of Carmichael's *Who's Who in Major League Baseball* and a cap that day. He took good care of me. He was a wonderful man.

Uncle Ernie, who one day would also become my step-father also took me to a Phillies game in that same time frame and seemed to know a bunch of those players too. Same locker room, different cast of characters. I loved their red, white and blue uniforms and was thrilled when the current Phillies resumed their use as their daytime home uniform.

Hank Sauer (1953 Topps card) quieted a heckler.

One day at a Phillies-Cubs game at Shibe Park some loud mouthed jerk a few rows behind us started heckling Cubbie outfielder Hank Sauer. "Sauer, you stink," he yelled and then added, "And you have a big nose". (In the interest of accuracy, Sauer did have a big nose.)

This clown kept the heckling up all game, until late in the contest when Sauer launched a monster homerun off Phils pitcher Curt Simmons in to the left field stands to give Chicago a lead – and the win.

When Sauer crossed the plate, instead of going to the dugout, he walked directly to where we were seated, stared at the heckler and said, "How'd you like that you (expletive deleted)?" The heckler was quiet, he had no reply.

Chapter XIX - Ten months until Christmas

The twins were born on February 25 – which meant that they had exactly ten months to go before their first visit from St. Nicholas. I'm glad they picked the 25th as an arrival date – my birthday is also the 25th, albeit September.

Brett said, "I can't wait, they'll be fun to have at Christmas". And he's right. In the Taylor Family Christmas is always a big day.

My Mother loved Christmas. As she grew older she delighted in buying presents, presents and more presents for her kids and grandchildren. One or two presents weren't ever enough – ten or more was more like it.

Mom began buying presents for next Christmas about two weeks after the current Christmas was in the books.

They weren't big presents but there were lots of them – and it became a Taylor family ritual that lasts to this day. What happened was that you would sit around and open one present, in turn. There was no tearing of paper in a mad frenzy; Mom insisted that things be done in an orderly manner.

But one year – the year my Dad died – Christmas almost didn't make it to our house and it took all the resources of a small boy to make it happen.

Chapter XX - The Glenside Kid Saves Christmas

It's December 1949 and it's the first Christmas since my Dad died. Mom had her hands full because not only did she have me to worry about she, somehow, wound up with her mother, Nanny (Irma) Roth, as a resident on Oak Road too.

Later in life that scenario truly annoyed me. There was my widowed Mom, age 40, with the expenses of running a single-parent household and her seven siblings, all better off than her, played pass-the-buck and dumped her ailing mother on her as well.

It was explained to me that since my Mom and Uncle Rudy were Nanny's only "real children" it came down to the two of them. Of course that was sheer nonsense – Irma helped raise them all - and when the siblings sold off her house on Limekiln Pike for a fish cake in the late 40's, all Mom got was the old lady – the rest of them picked off the furniture, the antiques (that Mom often showed me, especially at the Miller and Jenkins homes) and then they whacked up the sale price, meager as it was among all eight. It was a crummy thing to do and since Uncle Rudy was a struggling bread man living in West Oak Lane with three kids of his own, Mom won (lost?) the lottery.

9 year-old Teddy decides to tackle the holiday himself.

So Christmas, 1949, was looking pretty grim. Mom was deeply depressed over losing her husband and I'm sure I was a handful too. I was nine, what did you expect? Her mother was quite arthritic and had a hard time getting around. It was something less than a daily festival at 338 Oak Road.

It was getting close to Christmas and we had no tree, no decorations, not much of anything that would suggest that Santa Claus would soon pay us a visit. It really looked like he was taking the year off from the Taylor family.

The Glenside Kid

On Oak Road outdoor lighting displays were unheard of, but each home did put one green and one red bulb in their porch light receptacles. How they all got it right was a mystery, but everyone seemed to do it.

With two weeks to go to the big day, it looked like the two porch lights were going to be it as far as Christmas decorations at our house. And so I took matters in to my own hands. I still had some birthday money – I was always a saver – and I marched off to Glenside to personally rectify the lack of Christmas decorations.

I was just a kid but I knew exactly what I was going to do.

First I went to Ronnie's 5 & 10 in the heart of town and looked around for something that would add a festive look to our living room. I found it, too. It was a little plaster Manger scene and it came with all the people – and animals – necessary. I paid for it, they put it in a box and I marched home. I took it to my room and didn't tell Mom or Nanny Roth that I had it.

Next I headed back to Glenside were I noticed they were selling Christmas trees at Riley's Esso gas station near the elementary school. Since I had blown most of my bankroll on the Manger scene I'd need to be careful with my tree selection. I also felt that I would need to use my best negotiation skills.

I picked a regular sized tree, much taller than me, and asked the man in charge "how much?" I flinched when he then quoted a price – and I put it back. This scenario repeated itself as I went looking for even scroungier tall trees – and even they still cost too much.

But the guy selling the trees must have taken pity on pathetic little me because he steered me toward a beautifully shaped tree, albeit no taller than I was. "I can let you have this beauty for a buck," he said. I had a buck, that was it. I replied, "Okay but can you throw in some of those greens laying there?" And that's what they were, just branches off of other trees, and they were just laying there. He smiled and said, "Sure, I can do that". And so I had both a tree and materials to make a wreath for the front door.

My Mom later told me that she happened to be looking out the front door and saw me trudging up the street, dragging the tree with one hand, holding a load of greens in the other. She said it made her very happy and, all at once, she said she got the Christmas spirit. Later she told me that, I guess losing her husband wasn't exactly something to inspire a lot of holiday good will.

We dug out the old Christmas tree ornaments that were in the attic from the year before and put the little tree on a table in the living room. The Manger scene was placed on the mantel piece. Mom wrapped a red ribbon around the greens, hung a few Christmas balls on them and hung them from the door. My American Flyer trains circled a small platform in the living room. Christmas had found the Taylor family after all.

I don't exactly remember what I gave her – or she gave me – that Christmas, but I do remember that we were very happy, even my grandmother. It was us against the world and we were willing to play it that way. My Mom and I always had a special bond. She was a remarkable lady. A year later Nanny ended up in a nursing home in Wyncote and passed in 1951.

The Manger scene, by the way, makes an appearance every year in my house. It is a cherished part of the holiday season and lets me recall when we didn't have much – but shared a lot of love.

The Glenside Kid

Chapter XXI – We've always been joiners

My wife Cindy and I often go out to dinner, and this one Friday night we headed to the neighborhood bar& grille. It's now called Snavely's and is run by my boyhood friend, a guy who we nicknamed "Snavely" as kids. It's a real local hangout, loads of home towney ambiance, you get great food and you always meet folks there that you know.

As you enter the place the dark mahogany bar runs the length of the left half of the two-store- front building on the main drag in town. When Snavely's father bought it right after World War II it was strictly a gin mill with a smaller bar and a dozen stools and all the local drunks could be found there. Over the years, when business improved, his old man bought the flower store next door, enlarged the kitchen and expanded it in to eating establishment as well..

It's dimly lit, there's a full mirror behind the bar – that allows you to actually watch yourself get drunk - and all kinds of Phillies, Eagles, Flyers and Sixers sports memorabilia adorns the wall. Slats from a couple of Shibe Park seats add to the décor. Tables and booths are lined along one wall, the kitchen is in the back and tables, for those more interested in dining than drinking, fill up the other half. TV's hang from several spots on the wall, all of them showing sports events, if there are any, or news shows otherwise.

The place is loaded with Glenside memorabilia as well, including signs from many beloved, usually, defunct businesses. There are class pictures from many of the local schools – Glenside, Glenside-Weldon, Thomas Williams, Abington, Cheltenham, St. Luke's, Bishop McDevitt - and, among the photographic maze, are a few that I appear in.

Snavely, real name Dillon O'Malley, is 100% Irish so, of course each year St. Patrick's Day at the bar is like a combination of Christmas, New Year's Eve and the 4th of July all rolled in to one.

The Glenside Kid

If you can even get in the door you've done something. Getting out, later, is another challenge – and getting out reasonably sober seldom happens.

As a kid, sometimes after school I'd hang out in the back of the place with Snavely (and his brother Pig) playing with the dart board, watching the 12-inch Emerson TV and feeling like big shots. In the interest of full disclosure, Pig (real name Sean) was not fat, but was kind of sloppy, and today he is a college professor at an Ivy League university. I guess he now goes by Dr. Pig. Snavely's old man would pay the three of us a couple of bucks to come there on Saturday mornings and help clean up the place. Friday was always a big night at their bar and every couple of Saturday mornings we'd also have to dislodge some clown passed out or hung over from the night before.

As usual while we awaited dinner we encountered a few friends – one now golf pro at the local country club - and Cindy was off and rolling telling them all about the twins. That's the kind of place this is – still one of the town's social hubs.

Snavely brought us our dinner that was comprised of two O'Malley's –his specialty, a thin-sliced roast beef and cheese sandwich on a Kaiser roll, with his special horse radish sauce – and as he spread the food before us he asked me if I was still a member of the Philadelphia A's Historical Society. "My old man loved the A's, him being Irish like Connie Mack and all," he said, "I wish he had lived long enough to join the club."(Actually Mr. O'Malley has been dead for decades.) I told him I was still a member, but no longer all that active.

"Congrats on the twins," he said, "have a beer on me". I was floored. Snavely, who still has the first buck he ever earned, was never noted for his generosity so the twins must have impressed him.

Cindy chimed in that twins ran in both our families – her father had twin brothers, my mother also had twins in her family. Brett's wife also came from a family with twins in their history. It

The Glenside Kid

would have almost been a surprise if someone in our family didn't end up with twins.

"Maybe you guys should get them to join some kind of twins club," the ever alert Snavely opined.

The Taylor's have actually always been joiners – my dad especially. He was a Boy Scout, a Mason, active in the church and an Army vet.

I've been a member of the Rotary Club, Sigma Delta Chi fraternity, countless sports collector club and professional organizations, the Presbyterian Church and on and on.

And so it's reasonable to believe that the newest and smallest Taylor's will be joiners, one day too.

Snavely laughed and said, loud enough for everyone in the bar to hear, "Didn't you once belong to a gang?" And the answer was yes. I recall, very vividly, the first organization I ever joined – and it was indeed "gang".

Chapter XXIII - The Kid Joins a gang

In my neighborhood, when I was just a little guy the "Black Devils" were the most fearsome gang known to man or beast. At least they were if you were ten and lived on Oak Road. The very name sent shivers up your backbone.

The "Black Devils" originally had a club house about seven or eight houses away from my house on the opposite side of my street. It was behind Tommy King's garage as a matter of fact. If accuracy is important it was actually behind Julia and Herb King's garage. I think it was made of scraps of wood and nailed-on tar paper.

Before you get the wrong idea about the nature of my childhood – what with gangs and all – let me set the scene. The location was purely suburban – almost country.

But I digress. My street was bordered on the north by Limekiln Pike and a vast open field that was once the Kenworthy Estate farm and the site of World War II Victory Gardens. It was bordered to the south by Springhouse Lane and my elementary school. Behind it was Harrison Avenue, in front of it was a neat, very dense, woods, complete with creek and wildlife. All now gone, by the way, felled by "progress".

Eddie Cliff and the Black Devils

The period is the late 1940's, the early 1950's and the leader of this terrible, fearsome gang was Eddie Cliff who was, at best, 13 or 14. His younger brother Richard, a year older than me, was one of my best friends – and they had a little sister, Karen, who always wanted to be included in our adventures but seldom actually was. But we were, in the eyes of Eddie and Tommy and their intimidating hoard of ruffians, just the little pestery kids.

Not being able to sit before a TV from morning to night – we didn't have one in our house and I recall about three in the whole

The Glenside Kid

neighborhood – we had to come up with our own forms of amusement and whatever germs of adventure we plucked from the Saturday matinees at the Keswick or the Glenside movie theaters or from our favorite comic books or radio shows.

Imagination was in great supply in those days. It was well honed from listening to your favorite adventure stories – *The Lone Ranger, Sky King, Tom Mix, Bobby Benson and the BRB Ranch, Inner Sanctum, Gangbusters* - on the radio and filling in the visuals with your own imagination. I would, sometimes, sit at the kitchen table listening to my favorite shows and drawing pictures of what I heard. The paper I drew on was often the inside of folded open Christmas cards or old letterhead from Mom's friend and our neighbor Mrs. Mahwinney.

It only seemed natural that the biggest and oldest kid on the block would head up the "Black Devils" and that mantel was worn by Edna and Al Cliff's eldest son, Eddie. (Edna, by the way, lived to be 100 years old – the last of my mother's close friends - and the last time I spoke with her she sounded the same as she had when I was a little kid.)

Now I'm not sure what the gang really did, but I know that all the bigger kids in the neighborhood were in it and the little kids (me, Richard, John Ewing, Jimmy Hager, Snavely O'Malley) were not. Usually when we were playing baseball in my driveway and when we least expected it, the Black Devils would come screaming down the street and, generally, scare the crap out of us. We'd all run for cover and hoped they'd go away. And they usually did, laughing as they went, usually confiscating anything we dropped during our panic driven retreats. I really hated those guys.

In the woods across the street from my house was a thicket of small scrub pines where the Black Devils had moved their fortress after Eddie and Tommy had an unexplained falling out. I don't know what caused the rift, but Eddie left the fold and took most of the gang with him. I think Tommy and big Albert Haynes were the only ones left behind.

Their break-up was my big break. Tommy asked me to join his new gang. Imagine that? I was the second oldest of the little kids and, for some reason, was seen as a leader of the new breed. I still didn't know what gangs did, but I was now a member and allowed in Tommy's tar paper headquarters. I don't even recall the name of Tommy's new gang. A friend recently suggested it was the "Red Devils" but I think that was a vacuum cleaner or something. I recall having Red Rascal roller skates, but that's another story. I'll get to them later.

I do remember that Tommy's clubhouse had a radio and that actually worked and all sorts of weapons – spears, sling-shots and even a Daisy Red Ryder air rifle. If someone invaded us we were prepared to repel them with extreme daring and force.

I've joined a number of clubs in my life. I've been in the Rotary Club, Sigma Delta Chi – a professional society, even country clubs like Edgemont and Meadowbrook and being a member of something is what people like to do. So joining Tommy's gang was, in a sense, my first club membership. It was such a great feeling. I was allowed in to the clubhouse of this feared gang. I tried to explain that to my Mom but she thought I was a little nutty. Sometimes parents just don't get it.

Anyway Tommy had a project in mind. Quite simply, he wanted revenge and his goal was to destroy Eddie's new Black Devil's clubhouse. As I recall it now, Eddie's new digs were just barely a tent. Actually it was really some canvas draped over tree limbs and a few blankets and stuff.

After careful planning we chose a time for the attack. It was a summer morning and, as I remember it, Eddie was supposed to be attending summer school. We had some good intelligence, we thought. Richard, Eddie's younger brother, was also now in our gang. Eddie was such an elitist he wouldn't even let his own little brother join the Black Devils.

The Glenside Kid

The appointed day came and we crept through the woods, each of us heart-poundingly nervous as cats. But life didn't really get any better than this, if you know what I mean.

There were five of us. Tommy, me, Richard, Snavely and David Gillum (who, I mentioned earlier, and who later became a well-known and respected physician in upstate Pennsylvania, having somehow managed to live down this experience).

I slowed us down a bit when I fell in to the creek. We were always doing that, by the way. This creek seemed to suck kids in to it. I also had an unhealthy fear of quicksand and knew it was only a matter of time before I succumbed to that. (The quicksand paranoia was fostered by watching too many jungle serials on Saturdays at the movies.) I knew that my Mom would not be happy that my new sneakers and socks were soaking wet, but, hey that was life. I'd deal with that later.

So on we went.

Finally we got to the Black Devils headquarters and were relieved to find that nobody was home. Of course we already knew that, but I guess we really didn't trust our intelligence reports.

It took such a short time to trash the clubhouse that we were all kind of disappointed. To be honest, there wasn't much to trash. But we totaled it and left just a pile of rubble. As I recalled we all cackled like the fiends in the movies as we did our dirty deed.

Feeling like the Kings (no pun intended) of the neighborhood that we now knew ourselves to be we marched triumphantly back to our headquarters – only to find out that, somehow, the Black Devils had figured out our plans and had paid a reciprocal visit to us. Our clubhouse was reduced to ruins. Even the radio was busted. There was no clear-cut victor here. Both gangs were clubhouse-less. Strangely neither was ever rebuilt. I think that episode ended the Oak Road gang era. New temptations – like girls, baseball and cars – loomed on the near horizon.

It was never clear if Eddie had skipped school that day or what. We always suspected that Richard was the mole and had let him in our little secret, blood being thicker than water and all that, though he always denied it.

Justice among kids has a strange way of manifesting itself.

Those were the days.

Chapter XXIII - The weatherman cuts us a break

How many times have you allowed the TV weatherman to influence what you were going to do? The paranoia that they can generate with the simple word "snow" or "severe weather" drives people to do irrational things. Onetime a TV weathercaster (John Bolaris, Channel 10) in Philly forecast the blizzard of the century and was so frightening with his predictions that most school districts in the entire region cancelled classes before the first flake hit the ground. Of course it never snowed and most kids in the region got the day off anyway. Not long afterward Bolaris, the focus of endless scorn, took a job in another city.

We left Snavely's and headed home. The radio called for freezing rain. Both Cindy and I said, "I wonder what it'll really do?"

But when the due date for the twins was first announced – March 11 – I remember saying to Brett, "If I were a betting man, I'd put a lot of money on the worst blizzard of the year for that date".

He agreed stating that they his luck ran he'd probably have to hire a snowplow to get he and Colleen to the hospital. The year before, on March 12, we had almost a foot-and-a-half of snow. The odds were not in his favor.

But February 25 dawned – and with it came precipitation. But it was rain, though quite heavy, anyone with any sense can navigate some rain.

We actually did drive through a nasty, wind-blown, rainstorm on the way to the hospital, but by the time we hit Doylestown the sun was out – and the twins arrived in sunshine.

"I loved snow as I kid," I said to Brett, "But now can't stand the thought of it." He agreed.

But there was a time when it played right in to my finances.

Chapter XXIV- Let it $now

The old song "Pennies from Heaven" told us that every time it rained it rained pennies from Heaven. Well, if you were a kid growing up in the 1950's in Glenside every time it snowed it snowed profits from Heaven, at least it did for the guys who called Oak Road and Harrison Avenue home.

People still go to the store to buy milk and bread with every snow forecast and the folks at Lowes and Home Depot note, with gladness, that each snow brings additional sales of shovels and salt. My snow shovel has lasted at least 15 years through lots and lots of snowstorms, how is it that people feel the need to buy a new one with each blizzard? Do they throw the old ones away or what?

As a boy I rooted openly for snow. It was a guaranteed source of revenue. With my pals Jimmy, John, Snavely and Chuck the first item of business was always pushing cars up Limekiln Pike. It was steep, cars couldn't gain traction, we got fifty cents to get them going. It never occurred to us that if the car slid backward we could be crushed. Hey a half-a-buck is a half-a-buck. Risks? They don't exist for kids, we were immortal…gonna live forever.

Once the morning rush hour cleared and the supply of motorists declined we grabbed our snow shovels and began the most rewarding part of the storms – clearing off sidewalks and driveways. I don't think the cold really bothered us. I never remember, as a kid, coming in from the snow because I was cold.

It's hard to find kids willing to shovel your walks now-a-days. Contractors with plows on their trucks and snow blowers in the back have pretty much ended that economic bonanza for kids. I have a guy who comes to my house to shovel now – once it passes five inches – and it sets me back a hundred bucks each time he appears.

But in our day we could, sometimes, collect two (maybe even three) times for clearing the same sidewalks. We realized that

The Glenside Kid

if we really hustled we could get the whole thing clean, collect our money and be off before the township snow plow came down the street and dumped street snow all over their sidewalks and sealed off the access to their driveways.

One particularly large snowfall came and my Pop spent half the morning clearing the walk and our driveway. No sooner was he done than a snow plow came along and covered it all. Pop was so frustrated he yelled words I didn't know existed in his vocabulary and hurled his snow shovel at the truck itself. Undaunted the plow continued along its merry way.

The 1950 Ford covered with a March, 1956 snowfall

I had a 1950 Ford when I was 16. It was a stick shift and it would go anywhere. I learned that when it snowed you had to put the chains on – and I got very good at doing that. I'd jack that baby up, slap on my chains and be good to go anyplace. Of course if a link broke you ran the risk of doing damage to your car as a hunk of broken chain took a whack at it with every revolution of the tire.

One of the other great things about snow was the recreational aspect of it. Every one of us owned a sled – mine was an American Flyer – and a good snow meant that Lismore Avenue, two blocks away, would be closed to traffic. Lismore was the steepest street in the area and cars would get halfway up and then slide back down. So, before long, the Cheltenham Police would put saw horses across the top of it – at Limekiln Pike and the bottom of it – Spring House Lane.

We'd trudge up Limekiln Pike, dragging out sleds behind us, and then at the top of Lismore we were ready for a great ride. And the more kids that rode down it, the better it got – like a mountain ski run.

Our sled runners would be all soaped up – it made them faster – and down we'd go. And the barrier at Lismore and Spring House was just something to slip under. In fact a good run from the top of Lismore would take you down the hill, a right turn on Spring House, past Harrison and you'd wind up at the foot of Oak Road. What a ride! Of course you didn't do many of them because the return walk – back three blocks and up the hill - was a killer.

When the new Glenside School was built on Limekiln Pike we'd also sled down the hills there. They were good hills, but just a short run until you collided with a chain link fence unless you did some fancy steering. Life was good.

One of the transient Oak Roaders (people who lived there during my childhood but not for long), Frank Hudson, worked at the Cheltenham Mall and drove his Volkswagen Beatle (rear engine, excellent in snow, by the way) to work and then home in the evening for dinner. One day it snowed like mad and Frank went to work as usual. Late in the day he arrived home for dinner to find that a snowplow had closed off his driveway. He got out of the car, extracted a shovel from the back seat and dug his way in.

While he was eating dinner the plow came by again and, again, closed off his driveway. Upon leaving Frank, undaunted,

The Glenside Kid

shoveled his way out again. As luck would have it as he walked to the garage to put his shovel away, the snow plow came by a third time and plowed the driveway shut. He finally got the message. He went in to the house, called his workplace, and told them he wasn't coming back.

When I was in high school, the very same Cheltenham Mall – Gimbels was the anchor store - played a role in the worst day in the life of a close friend. We had a huge blizzard, in February 1958, – so huge that I got stranded, as luck would have it, at my girl friend's house for almost three days. I loved the snow that time. She lived near the mall. For two nights I slept in the waiting room of her father's dentists office – she slept three floors away. It didn't matter.

My friend Merritt, who lived near my girlfriend, offered to drive me home on day three – when my welcome at the Hudson home was fast wearing out - and I accepted. He wanted to stop off at the mall to get something – he was always buying "something" - and so we went there. He parked the car and soon we encountered a our classmate friend, Joe Peterson, who was driving his father's brand new silver '58 Chevy.

Lots of snow had been plowed in to large piles all around the mall lot and Joe told us that it was "all kinds of fun" to drive your car at a high rate of speed in to one of them. "The snow scatters and it looks neat," he laughed, he said he'd already done it a couple of times there. Merritt and I both thought he was a little goofy, but we smiled as he told his story.

Merritt passed on the thrill of it all, and then Joe uttered the words, "Let me show you what it looks like" and before we could say "Jack Robinson" (or even Joe Peterson) he had hopped in to his car and was making a beeline for a huge pile of snow in the far distant corner of the lot.

The next thing we knew there was this big crashing sound, metal ripping, glass breaking and then the car shot backwards, the front totaled and it was smoking like a locomotive. Joe was bloodied, but okay. Seems he had mistaken a stone wall covered by snow for a drift made completely of snow. His father was quite furious when he got the news, Joe was lucky to be alive. Merritt drove me, and Joe, home. Joe's father's car was a total wreck. The next time we saw him driving a car it was a clunker and one that he bought for himself.

The Glenside Kid

Chapter XXV - The first day of the rest of their lives

You've heard the sages say, "Today is the first day of the rest of your lives", but for the Taylor twins February 25, 2011 really was.

The entire new four-member Taylor family - Brett II and Lily, his 30-second older sister - were visiting our house for dinner one Sunday while Big Brett was working on installing my new computer – he loves working on computers.

Colleen reminded us that Brett had raved about the food at the hospital where the kids were born. I told her that I thought that the pricey lunch I had in the hospital cafeteria on the day they were born was the worst I'd ever attempted to eat, so I didn't eat much of it. Were the meal to make you sick, however, I couldn't think of a better place to be.

I told her that the reason we hadn't stayed longer the day the twins were born was that we were hungry and couldn't face yet another meal there. So late that afternoon we said our goodbyes and opted to head for home.

Leaving the hospital we drove to the Rt. 202 by-pass, segued to Easton Road through Warrington and came upon the "Long Horn Steak House". We went there for dinner, we were both hungry and elated about the kiddies. I love the décor of the place, especially for a cowboy aficionado like me. It's ersatz "old west" but it works.

Next door is one of those multi-screen movie houses where, if you can't find at least one movie you like, you aren't trying, and where you'll spend more money on candy and pop corn than on your actual ticket.

I was a movie buff as a kid and still like the older flicks best of all. Turner Classic Movies is a favorite and so is Encore's Westerns Channel. But what I do miss, and seldom see, are the old serials that were a staple of the Saturday matinees of my boyhood.

The Glenside Kid

Also the flicks that fostered my first raging passion for someone exotic of the opposite sex.

Chapter XXVII - Nyoka, Queen of the Jungle

I always loved adventure and I loved living it from the confines of the seats at either the Glenside or Keswick theatres every Saturday afternoon. The standard fare was a cartoon, a newsreel, the previews, a cowboy picture and a serial.

We all loved the cartoons, except for those stupid follow the bouncing ball sing-a-longs, we tolerated the newsreels and previews, loved the cowboy pictures as Hopalong Cassidy, Roy Rogers, Gene Autry, Wild Bill Elliot, Bob Steele, Lash LaRue and others of heroes dispatched the bad guys week-after-week.

I really liked Tim Holt westerns (his father had been silent film cowboy Jack Holt) and his sidekick Chito Rafferty (played with eloquent style by the handsome Richard Martin). Most sidekicks were old and/or goofy (Gabby Hayes, Fuzzy St. John, Pat Buttram, the magnificent and multi-talented Smiley Burnett, Andy Clyde), but Rafferty had the qualities that made him a solid second lead. The bad guys knew that when Chito had the drop on them they'd better not make a move, ditto with Hopalong Cassidy's sidekick Russell Hayden who played a character named "Lucky" Jenkins. Gabby Hayes – who "side kicked" most of the western stars - or the other comic relief guys might just as likely shoot themselves in the foot and let the bad guys escape.

But with it all it was the serials that provided the entertainment designed to get you back in the theatre again next week. Every episode ended with the hero or heroine in some grave, life threatening, danger. You had to pop for another quarter next week to see if they survived. And, by the way, they always did.

The first true love crush of my life was *Nyoka the Queen of the Jungle*. The lovely Nyoka, officially dubbed "The Jungle Girl", was always getting chased by a huge animal, tied to something, tossed off something or stuck in quicksand and some guy always had to rescue her. As I got older I figured out that I really liked it when Nyoka (either actress Frances Gifford or Kay Aldridge, they both played the part in a serial and I don't recall which one of them was actually my initial heart throb) fell in to something wet because it made her skimpy costume cling to her in ways that little boys of all ages could admire.

The nice thing about movie serials, at least from the standpoint of the theatre owner, was that they could be recycled as kids grew up. I didn't learn, until much later in life, that Nyoka's exploits were actually filmed when I was just a baby – and here, at age 11 or 12, my hormones were racing over someone who hadn't run from a character actor in a bad looking gorilla costume in over a decade.

The first passion of my life, Nyoka the Jungle Girl

Gene Autry's *Phantom Empire* serial was actually his first major role in the mid-1930's and so when we were seeing it at the Keswick in the early 1950's it was almost two decades old. We didn't know how dated it was, that the robots looked stupid by today's standards, all we knew was that it was a cool adventure.

The Glenside Kid

We also watched Buster Crabbe, with a bad blonde dye-job in his hair, playing *Flash Gordon* and we both hated and were scared to death of his nemesis *Ming the Merciless* (what a great name for a villain). There were really bad looking ill-fitting costumes in the 1939-made *Batman* serial, but we all loved Kirk Allyn's portrayal of *Superman*. To me he was always the real (or is it "reel"?) Man of Steel. George Reeves, the TV version, was an imposter, though a pretty good one. Reeves, however, did star in a serial *The Adventures of Sir Galahad*. Thanks to Reeves we had a run of Knights of the Roundtable adventures that one year.

There were also lots of takes on *Zorro*. I recall at least three such serials. One was *Zorro* himself, one was called *Son of Zorro* and the third *The Mark of Zorro* was about Zorro's daughter. As I recall, *Son of Zorro* didn't bother with a horse, he rode a motorcycle.

The Keswick theatre also had this penchant for games. Among other things they killed time. The one I hated the most was called "the shoe scramble" and every kid was supposed to take off their shoes and toss them in a pile on the stage. When the usher blew a whistle the first kid to retrieve his pair of shoes from the pile won a free ticket to next weeks' matinee. It was grim, limbs were almost lost. I hated the scramble and after one or two of them I refused to take part – the grand prize for being the first one to find your own shoes was a bag of popcorn. There were actually kids, as I recall, who went home with mismatched shoes. And for reasons I could never fathom, there were always shoes left over. How did that happen?

Each week when the hero-du jour's picture came on the kids in the audience screamed their approval. It didn't matter who it was, as long as it was Roy, Gene, Hoppy, Wild Bill or someone of that ilk. One Saturday they pulled a fast one on us and sprung a mystery movie on us – starring, of all people, singer Dick Haymes. I was the lone kid screaming my approval and I felt like an idiot. The movie stunk, too.

One Saturday afternoon I watched the scariest movie of my life. I'm probably 12 and the movie was *Abbott and Costello meet Frankenstein*. Every movie monster there ever was – Wolfman, Dracula, Jekyll and Hyde and, of course, Frankenstein himself were in it.

Abbott and Costello were comedians, but this movie gave me nightmares. Later in life I bought a VHS tape of it and it still was frightening and I understood why it scared me so as a small boy.

Those matinees provided us with adventures for a whole week until the next Saturday when we re-lived and re-invented ourselves once again.

With all the niche' TV stations that exist today you'd think someone would launch a "Serials Channel" so I could get reacquainted with Nyoka, Son of Zorro and the rest of my childhood heroes.

Chapter XXVII – Setting up a legacy –

Once the 2011 Topps complete baseball sets hit the market I will be buying one for Brett II. It's something I always said I'd do if I ever got a grandson and now that I've got one he can count on a complete baseball set every season for as long as I can buy them for him.

When I told my wife this she said, "What about Lily?" And I told her that if Lily wanted a set I'd get her one too. Yes, I know it isn't fair, but one of the great passions in my life has been baseball cards.

Baseball cards were our currency as kids. "I'll swap you my Marv Rotblatt for your Willie Mays", was not uncommon as knowledgeable kids did their best to snooker their less informed playground mates.

I once helped create – and then ran - the largest Baseball Card Show in America (founded at Spring Garden College in 1975) and have been a baseball card hobby columnist for several national magazines and The Philadelphia Daily News. The "Philly Show" as it was known achieved national stature in 1971 when I presided over an auction of three 1952 Topps Mickey Mantle cards – and sold all three for $9,000. The story went coast-to-coast after "The New York Times" broke it".

For almost eight years I worked for a baseball card manufacturer – Fleer – and if that wasn't living the dream of a lifelong card collector I don't know what is.

To this day I still enjoy busting a pack of baseball cards. Like it or not, Brett II is getting baseball cards.

Chapter XXIII- The baseball card "Kid"

I bought my first pack of baseball cards in 1948 at the White Pharmacy in Glenside – and I was hooked. To this day I cannot stand an unopened pack of cards. I need to tear off the wrapper and find out who is pictured inside. The enclosed gum in those days was incidental.

In that first pack of black-and-white cards was a Phillies player named Emil "The Antelope" Verban. But really he probably wasn't even a Phillie when I got the card because they had traded him to the Chicago Cubs in mid-season. A's players Ferris Fain, Eddie Joost and Barney McCoskey joined Phillies Dutch Leonard and Verban in the set.

The cards were small, black-and-white, and a whole set was 48 cards. I think I got most of them that year – certainly I have all of them now. Collecting baseball cards has been a lifelong passion for me and with it some good times and some not so good.

Once the bug bit I had to have all of the cards that I could get. Leaf Gum was also producing cards in 1948 and there were playing card sized black-and-white ones that someone told me Bond Bread had issued the year before. With a little digging I got some of them, along with some Bowman's and some Leaf cards and cobbled together a pretty neat collection.

By 1949 baseball cards were a big deal. The colorful Bowman set included 240 cards and those Leaf cards were back again too. Honestly as I look at those cards today I realize how ugly they were. Actually they were black-and-white pictures that had been poorly colored. But who cared? Not me.

By 1950 I was known all around Glenside Elementary School as "The King of Baseball Cards". Every cent I had went in to them. I was a good flipper – a matching game we played with cards - and would take on all challengers. I'd then trade my winnings for other cards that I needed. Once I traded a Del Ennis

The Glenside Kid

card to Robert Westerman for 45 cards that I needed. Del was my favorite player and I hated to do it, but 45 cards for one? I'm not stupid. After school I walked down to Ronnie's 5&10 in Glenside, bought three nickel packs and, tah dah, found a Del Ennis. It was a good day for "the King".

1950 Bowman Baseball cards, they were my passion, left to right, Jim Konstanty, Andy Seminick, Robin Roberts, Del Ennis, Rich Ashburn. I was the "King of baseball cards" at Glenside Elementary

And then one Sunday the *Inquirer* magazine came and on the cover was a picture of Buddy Crowder, a kid at our school, and a story about baseball cards. Give me a break. Buddy Crowder? He was a piker, I was "the King". Not only that but the picture of Buddy had him wearing an old style red-and-blue Phillies cap when everyone with any knowledge of baseball at all knew that the 1950 Phillies were wearing a red cap with a white "P" and red pinstripes on their uniforms. It turned out that Buddy's old man knew somebody at the paper and they were doing a story about baseball cards and needed a picture of a kid.

I never forgave Buddy or the *Inquirer*, for that matter.

My friend Joe Whipple and I were ardent collectors. Joe (real name George) went on to become a cop in our township. We would trade and wheel and deal and both of us put together some pretty neat collections. Joe loved the Phillies. He lived with his Mom and his grandparents in a nice house on Harrison Avenue. I never did hear anything about his father.

At that time of my life I found myself in a bit of a dilemma. By rights I was an A's fan – having met Connie Mack and all that – but the 1950 A's were awful – on the way to losing 103 games - and the 1950 Phillies were making an unheard of run at the National League pennant. Soon my A's cap was replaced by a Phillies one. What can I say, typical of most Philadelphians, I became front runner.

Uncle Ernie took me to a bunch of games that summer – mostly the Phillies as I recall – and we went with his pals Joe Merklinger, Joe Bates and Matt Repinski. Four tough guys and me. Life was good.

I don't know how many games we actually saw – but there were a bunch of them – and we saw some pretty good players too including Stan Musial, Willie Mays and, of course, those Brooklyn Dodgers.

We went to at least two different games where the Phillies ace Robin Roberts squared off against Dodger ace Don Newcombe. Both men wore #36, both men could hit. They were some contests. Robbie won one of them by hitting a homerun. Unc also liked the Dodgers because they were loaded with stars – Jackie Robinson, PeeWee Reese, Duke Snider, Roy Campanella, and Gil Hodges. A fearsome club, for sure.

When the Phillies knocked off the Dodgers with a dramatic extra inning homerun by Dick Sisler in the last game of the season Unc assured me that he'd get us tickets. But all of his connections failed him, the ballpark seated something like 32,000 people and the last pennant in Philly was when the A's won it in 1931. Try as he might he turned up no tickets. The man was crest fallen.

The Glenside Kid

The 1950 Phillies were something special to Uncle Ernie and me

And then, as if the powers that be were playing a joke on him, his wife (my Aunt Florence) gets assigned by her employer, Western Union, to work the press box during the games at Shibe Park. Aunt Florence didn't even like baseball, Uncle Ernie was a wreck and was relegated to listening to the games on the radio. The Phillies were swept four-games-to-none, but we salved our wounds by remembering that at least they got there.

A black moment in my young life

Baseball cards also brought me one of the blackest moments of my childhood.

I collected all the brands of cards, Bowman, Topps, Berk Ross, Exhibits – I just loved the pictures of my idols. And one day, it was spring 1953, I was at Ronnie's 5&10 and I discovered cellophane packages of the 1952 Topps cards. Obviously the cards had been repackaged and were being liquidated and, best of all, they were cheap!

I went home and gathered up all my money and went back to Ronnie's and bought as many packs as I could afford. I took them home, sorted them out, and then headed back for more. But I made a mistake. I left the cards I had just purchased in my pockets.

I was standing there looking at more cello packs when this nasty lady who looked like she had been weaned on a pickle, hair in a tight gray bun, long non-descript gray or black dress, and really quite witchy-looking comes up to me, grabs me by the neck and says, "I caught you stealing". I was stunned. I had never stolen a thing in my life. I told her that. She laughed. "Don't lie to me you little creep," she cackled.

Next thing I know she takes all my cards from me and, literally, throws me out of the store saying "never come back here again you little criminal".

I was emotionally destroyed and surely not happy - and I ran all the way home. I'm 12 and am an accused criminal banned for life from my favorite 5&10. As I babbled on, tearfully, to my Mom about what happened she got angrier and angrier. She didn't take kindly to me being called a crook. So we hopped in the '40 Plymouth and drove back to Glenside.

Mom burst through the door like Elliot Ness used to do when he broke in to destroy the bad guy's stills. "I want to see the owner, right now!" she demanded – and kindly Mrs. Lodge came trotting over to us from somewhere saying "what's the problem?"

At that moment I spied the old witch who had confiscated my cards and pointed toward her. My mom picked up on that and said, "She's the problem and I want this resolved right now or I'm going to the police."

Mom explained in very harsh terms to Mrs. Lodge that I saved every nickel I had to buy baseball cards and she was there when I first came home and told her of my discovery of the 1952 cards. In fact she had given me a dollar to get more, she said.

"Did she see him steal the cards?" Mom demanded, and Mrs. Lodge looked at the harsh floor-walker who nodded that, well, she really hadn't exactly seen me steal the cards, but justified her actions and chirped, "But who expects a kid to have that many baseball cards?"

The Glenside Kid

Then Mom really lost it. She said, "forget the police", and then suggested that her childhood friend, J. Ernest Nachod, the lawyer in the bank building across the street, might enjoy suing Ronnie's 5&10's ass off for making false accusations. Hey, the lawyer card worked in 1953 just like it works today. Panic ensued. Mrs. Lodge was clearly losing it, too. She starts babbling on about how it was "an honest mistake" and that we had "over-reacted".

Over-reacted? Bad choice of words. Mom started for the door. "I'll see you in court," she said. It was one of those moments when I loved my mother more than I ever imagined.

At that point Mr. Lodge heard the threat and joined the fray. He was really annoyed, but clearly on our side. First he told his wife to "shut up" and then he told the old witch to give me my cards back – she still had them in the back of the store – and to give me my money back, too, and another ten packs of cards. He also forced her to apologize to me – and she did so reluctantly. You know, it was one of those half-assed apologies that aren't all that sincere. But the point had been made and I had a hundred more cards to play with.

We should have sued. I'll bet you Mr. Nachod would have enjoyed it.

Chapter XXIX – Helping their friend the dentist

Brett and Colleen have had a lengthy doctor-patient relationship with Dr. Timothy Chaykosky, the proprietor and dentist-in-chief of "All Smiles Dental" in Ambler PA.

When the twins were born Dr. Tim thanked them for the "potential new clients". Brett, at the time, pointed out that the twins had no teeth at the moment.

Brett, probably thanks to my paranoia and the scars of my youth, was never big on going to the dentist. But as a young man just out of Gwynedd Mercy College he noticed that his teeth hurt him a lot and assumed that, just maybe, he had neglected them far too long. My Mom always used to say "Be true to your teach or they'll be false to you". Corny, yes, but on target.

Opting to save, rather than lose, his teeth he went on a search for a dentist and found one only a few blocks away from a house he was renting in town at the time.

It's on the second floor of a building, right around the corner from the Ambler movie theatre and right across the street from the Presbyterian Church. You can both get your teeth fixed and get saved on the same block.

Dr. Tim managed to save his teeth, albeit after a lot of work, and Brett became a disciple spreading the doctrine and telling everyone how great "All Smiles really was".

Before long Brett's friends and Colleen's family all joined the All Smiles cheering section and when our Huntingdon Valley-based dentist mysteriously closed his office and moved to Florida we signed up too. And for the first time in my life I actually don't mind going to the dentist.

That wasn't always the case, however.

The Glenside Kid

Chapter XXX – A fate worse than death

Once-a-year my Mom made me go to the dentist. I hated it, all kids hated it. I was afraid of the dentist and I just didn't want to go. I equated the word dentist with the words "great pain".

In those days, before flossing and fluoride and all that other preventative stuff, the motivating factor for going to the dentist was that you went only when you had a toothache. The current notion that your teeth have to be professionally cleaned every few months hadn't been thought of yet. In those days I figured that if my teeth didn't hurt I was simply wasting my time and my mom's money making that dreaded trip to the dentist's office.

The brothers Gage – George and Horace – were our longtime family dentists. Their offices were located in an office building that over-looked the in-bound side of the Glenside Reading Railroad station. The offices were on the second floor at the top of a very steep set of stairs. The hallway at the top was always dark. No light at all, or nothing much more than what trickled out of the clouded glass office doors. I always felt that a visit there and a climb up those steps was closely akin to what a convict must experience on his long walk to the electric chair.

The Gage brothers were old – at least they seemed old to me. But then everyone seemed old to me. Horace was very tall and reed thin. George was closer to average build. Both had white hair. Horace's was bushy, like Einstein, George's was thinning.

My mother would drive me to the dentist's office and drop me off while she went shopping at the Acme. It was agreed that she'd come to the waiting room when she was done if I already wasn't waiting for her on the sidewalk. I think the shopping thing was a ruse and that she didn't want to be anywhere near the dentist unless she really had to. Adults weren't that crazy about dentists either.

The Glenside Kid

This one day I went there, expecting to see Dr. George, but there was a sign on his door that said "Dr. George Gage is ill today, Dr. Horace Gage will see you". Oh crap, I thought. Now I was ill, too. I didn't like him even more than I didn't like his brother.

I walked in to Dr. Horace's office and it could best described as furnished in early Spartan. There were wooden hard-backed chairs in the waiting room – no sense in getting comfortable. The walls were colored a drab blue. There were no magazines, comics for kids or books to leaf through. The only thing on a beat up looking brown table was "The Holy Bible". Oh brother, I was in trouble and I knew in.

The door to his office was closed but I could hear the drill whirring and could only imagine how bad it probably was for the current victim, err patient.

I chose not to read the Bible, but rather just sit there and wait like any condemned man would. This particular day I was, maybe 12 or 13, but resolved to my fate.

About a half hour of my mind running amok over the pending horrors, Dr. Horace dismissed his current patient and said, "You must be Teddy," no kidding, who did he think I was? There was no lone else in the waiting room.

He ushered me in to his torture chamber (office) and had me climb in to his ancient splitting-leather padded dental chair. He quickly sticks a paper bib on me – to catch all the blood, I imagine – and starts poking and prodding around in my mouth. And, typical of all dentists everywhere since time began, he begins asking me questions.

I'd like to answer him, of course, but his fist is in my mouth along with some kind of thingy with a hook on it.

The Glenside Kid

"Aha," he chirps, "I found a cavity". Oh crap, I thought. And then he found another. He was having a big day; I wanted to be anywhere but there.

"I'll take care of both of them," he says, "I don't have anyone else scheduled this afternoon". Just my luck, I'm there for the duration, I think. Heck I even offered to come back some other time if he only wanted to do one today. He said, "No, we'll get them both right now".

Then he looks at me and says, "I could give you a shot of something to mask the pain, but you look like a brave little fellow and I figure you can handle it." I wanted to scream, "I'm a sissy, numb it you idiot", I thought that but my mother always taught me to be respectful of my elders – even those who were on the verge of inflicting serious pain on me.

So after he stuffs my mouth with rolls of cotton and digs around with another hooked thingy he says, "Okay let's get started". Cripes he wasn't even started yet. What was he doing looking for a gold mine in there?

Then he fires up the drill and I figure I'm doomed. Pain lurks. And he starts the drill in to my tooth. Presto, he hits a nerve. I flinch, in fact I gave out a muffled yell, but all that junk in my mouth quieted my screams. I was afraid I was going to die, then, again, I was afraid I wasn't.

He drills some more, obviously doing away with that nasty old cavity. He shoots water in to my mouth and, son-of-a-gun, the water hits the nerve and I get another jolt.

Dr. Horace then starts whipping up some gray concoction that will soon fill the hole he had drilled. He then pushes and prods it in to the spot where the cavity once resided – it makes a creaky, squeaky sound. He tells me to bite down and I do. My mouth won't close – the filling is too high. He scrapes some of it, tells me to bite down again. By now I'm an emotional wreck. I don't like this tall man. It was like being attacked by Ichabod Crane run amok.

But soon he has the filling smoothed out and tells me that my tooth is now "good as new". Sure it is, except now it has cement in it or something. I am spent and offer no resistance when he tackles the second cavity. In fact when he struck the nerve, as I knew he would, I was prepared and just flinched a little.

He repeated all the same exercises again. By now I think I know what going to Hell must be like and, at the same time, wondering where my mother is.

Dr. Gage finishes with me and, at the same time, my mom walks in.

"How is he doctor?" she asks.

"He was a brave soldier," he replies.

A soldier huh? Where is my Purple Heart? I was definitely wounded in action. What he gives me, instead, is a lolly pop. Imagine a dentist gives me something made of sugar. Of course, why not? I eat this baby and soon I have another cavity and I'll be back in his clutches once again.

Most kids that I grew up with had a basic distrust, if not fear, of the dentist and I think was justified. In fact it's a miracle that any of us even still have teeth.

My mother never made me go to Dr. Horace again. But I stuck with Dr. George until I graduated from high school. After that I never saw him again.

Chapter XXXI - Not much of a skater

The babies have a shot at having a sense of rhythm because their Grandmother, my wife, can flat out dance. I on the other hand, have always been, the proud owner of two left feet.

Perhaps my lack of cadence comes from the crummy roller skates I had as a kid. Maybe I was forever tainted by them. I know as a teenager we'd go on skate dates at the local rink and I would hold on for dear life and, eventually, take a pratfall. Ice skating? Are you kidding?

My wife Cindy, on the other hand, can dance, can skate and, I suspect, could probably have been a TV star on "Bandstand" had they ever given her a shot when she was a teenager. As a kid from South Philly's St. Maria Goretti High School, the part of the city where I think they invented dancing, she tried desperately to penetrate the inner sanctum of the clique that was the teen performers on Dick Clark's national TV show. She got close a couple of times, but never got in to the WFIL TV studios. It was their loss.

You name a legendary teen dance spot in Philly – Wagner's, Chez Vous - Cindy was there. Jerry Blavat? The Geator? She claims to have been to his first hop. She also lived for the nightly dances on the Wildwood Boardwalk at the Starlight Ballroom, where, ironically, Dick Clark was often the deejay.

She can still dance circles around people half her age – and I'm always proud to sit on the sidelines at wedding receptions as she dazzles them with her graceful moves and her well choreographed footwork.

Sometimes when we're driving some place the Sirius Satellite radio will play a tune from her teen years and she'll do the hand gesture parts of the dance even though she is seated.

Chapter XXXII - Red Rascal Roller Skates

How does the name Red Rascal Roller Skates grab you? If you are on the shady side of 60 it could recall wild memories of the past or, if you had a protected childhood, it might not grab you at all.

My childhood, at least a good many of the waking hours of it, was spent upon Red Rascal Roller Skates. Skates, incidentally, for which I invariably lost the key.

The big thing now is in-line skates, fancy, expensive things that people wear in the interests of physical fitness or simply being cool. But regular street roller skates faded because our suburban sprawl was built upon hills and dales more amenable to bicycles than skates. Hills and dales are hazardous to the health of even the best street skater.

But, getting back to my Red Rascals. These babies had bright red wheels, genuine ball-bearings inside and they guaranteed to make you about the fastest thing around. Greased lightning was a crawl compared to the way you were supposed to clip along on your Red Rascals.

It wasn't that I even liked having roller skates, but all the kids on our block had them and peer pressure being what it is – even when you are a kid – you traveled around on them.

I even recall the first pair of skates that my parents bought me during the Second World War and, because of the tight metal supply, the wheels were made out of wood. That's right, wooden-wheeled roller skates, and I gotta tell you, you didn't make much headway on them. They were a bad idea from day one and no one in their right mind could have believed that wooden wheels would work on concrete sidewalks. Because they didn't. What they did do was chip and soon you were laying, face down, on the sidewalk while all your friends went in to hysterics.

The Glenside Kid

Happily, for my roller skating career, the end of the War and the beginning of my elementary school coincided so that metal roller skates became available just at the time that I had to have them. I mean what self-respecting kid could go around on wooden-wheeled roller skates?

I mentioned before that roller skates became almost a part of your anatomy. A friend of mine told me that she used to skate down to the store for her mother, skate in through the door, and skate around the aisles doing the shopping and then skate though the checkout line and back out the door.

Kids hated to take off their skates because it was a lot of bother attached to your shoes as they were. Most of them couldn't take them off anyway if they didn't t have a key, and most kids managed to lose their keys shortly after they got their skates. Actually most skate keys fit most other skates – they weren't like car keys - so if you lost yours you could always bum one off Richard or Jimmy or Karen or Carol.

Once I lost my key – and all the neighborhood kids had already gone home. My Mom didn't like you to wear your skates in doors and when she called me for supper I was in a real dither. Should I cut off my feet? I wondered. And it was then that my sister Pat suggested, "hey dummy, just untie your shoes and step out of them". Amazing.

I was about as good at skating as I was at dancing. Other things were much more important – like baseball and everything associated with it. In my mind football and basketball were simply those sports that filled time between baseball seasons.

Chapter XXXIII - Wonder how the cats will like the twins?

One thing that was of some concern to Brett and Colleen was how their new twins would adapt to their old twins – and vice versa.

For close to seven years their only "children" were two Siamese cats named Maggie and Leopold. They were pedigreed litter mates and they were about six weeks old when they arrived in North Wales. It appeared that "Grand cats" were all we were getting from Brett and his wife, but then providence interceded and along came Brett II and Lily.

The Siamese cats were, to be blunt, pampered. They were their kitty cat children and were treated that way. They loved to sit on laps, loved to play, life for them was good. Maggie would leap in to Brett's arms and Leopold just loved it when you scooted him across the hardwood floors like a mop.

If you watched the Walt Disney film "Lady and the Tramp" you know what crummy publicity Siamese cats got and how people are naturally afraid of them. Take it from me, and we have their brother and sister (Casper and Wendy, litter mates from one litter later), they are big babies and wouldn't harm a fly.

My father-in-law declared "They have to get rid of those cats so they don't suffocate the babies". Never really a deep thinker, the patriarch of the tribe was simply mouthing long held myths about cats and babies. Brett Sr. noted there as about as much chance of getting rid of the cats as getting rid of the eldest family member (who, at this writing is 87).

I'm pleased to report that both sets of twins – cat and human – are getting along fine, though when the babies cry the cats tend to take off for safer, and quieter, surroundings.

The Taylor family has had a funny relationship with pets. When our kids were growing up they always wanted a dog – and we had a bunch of them. None, however, lasted long in our household

The Glenside Kid

for a myriad of reasons. One, a little white guy named Benji, had this penchant for running away from home with yours truly in hot pursuit. One day he ran away – I was at work - and no one else chased him. We never saw him again.

We had dogs with a kennel cough (annoying), one that chased cars (bad for his health), one that never got the idea of being house broken, and so on. In fact as my kids grew up the only successful pets were cats. And that probably explains why between my wife and I and our kids we own close to ten of them. Eight of them, by the way, are Siamese. We once had a Siamese named Suki who got to be 20-years-old.

But as a boy there was a very special dog in my life and if we ever do get another pooch it will be a Boston Terrier.

Chapter XXXIV - My best pet was half-a-dog

Growing up I had half-a-dog as a pet.

The obvious question is how do you have half-a-dog? And the answer, really, was quite simple. My boyhood dog was a Boston Terrier named Cookie. But Cookie also had another home; she was my Aunt Clare and Uncle Charlie's dog as well. We kind of shared her.

Every November my aunt and uncle departed for a long winter vacation in Florida and Cookie moved down the street to our house until they came home in April. And even when Cookie didn't actually live at our house I was usually the one who took her for a walk each day since they lived right up the street from us.

Cookie the Boston Terrier

Cookie was a very cool little dog. She also was extremely well trained. At night you would tell her to go to her little red metal box in the kitchen and she'd toddle off and get in. We kept it filled with soft blankets for her to snuggle in to. We would then put a small white fence across the entrance of the box and she would not come out. It never dawned on her that both sides of her box were wide open. She knew that the fence meant that she had to stay in the

The Glenside Kid

box. In the morning, when Mom came downstairs, she'd be in the box wiggling in her cute little way, wanting out in the worst way, but knowing she couldn't leave the box until the fence was removed.

Her daily chore was to wake me for school and she performed it well. The first thing Mom did was feed her. Every morning she ate a bowl of *Wheaties*. Why did she eat cereal? Well Uncle Charlie was a very good golfer and every time he got a hole-in-one or won a tournament he got a case of *Wheaties*. My uncle did not like that cereal, my cousins Buddy and Barbara didn't either. I thought they tasted dry. But Cookie loved it. Not "Breakfast of Champions", but the "Breakfast of Boston Terriers".

For dinner each evening she got a half-a-can of something called *Pard*. In fact it smelled pretty good and I always wondered what would happen if you spread it on a cracker and gave it to someone to eat. I wondered but I never did it.

Cookie could tell time, too. Pop came home every day at 4.15 PM and every day at that time the she would be waiting at the front door for him. He'd go have a beer and some snacks and the dog would get snacks too. Once Ernie decided to have some limburger cheese – the foulest smelling dairy product known to man – and we all left the house because it smelled so bad. All of us, that is, but Cookie. She and Pop sat in the kitchen their eating the rancid smelling cheese and having a grand old time of it.

Each morning Cookie would be attached to a run out back to do her business. One time it snowed so hard that we had to shovel a hole in the snow – sort of an igloo – so that she had a place to go. Cookie liked the igloo and on the back of a picture I found in a box in the attic my Mother had written, "...Notice Cookie's igloo, she climbs on top like a mountain goat".

Like most dogs, Cookie loved a good car ride and Mom would take her along whenever she could. Once Mom took the turn off Easton Road to Glenside Avenue a little too hard and Cookie went sailing out the window of the car.

"I've killed the dog," Mom thought, and quickly pulled over to the side of the road, afraid she'd find something awful. But what she found was Cookie sitting on the sidewalk at the corner waiting for her. Mom said that if dogs could talk she'd have probably said, "What the hell just happened?"

She was a great dog, and loved both of her families. She lived until I went away to college.

A more permanent pet, in that we had it 365-days-year, was Pete the Parakeet. I was never all that crazy about birds, but my mother liked them and decided that the very popular parakeet (it was a national craze in the 50's) would be perfect. They were supposed to talk; Peter, who had pretty blue feathers, never got the hang of it.

But Pete was okay. His biggest flaw was that he had this suicidal habit of flying in to the large mirror over our fireplace and knocking himself out. He crash, drop on the mantle piece and lay there. We'd pick him up, stick him back in his cage and in a while he'd be back singing as usual. He had a permanent scar on his head, right by his bill.

One day Pete hit the mirror, landed on the mantle and ended up buried in a box in the back yard. He had lived about three years.

There weren't a lot of pets in the neighborhood. I guess the residents had enough trouble just feeding their own kids. The few I recall were Boots the Cat, who belonged to the Cliff family and lived to be in his 20's. He was a tough old cat, prowled the woods across the street and, occasionally, came home looking like he had lost a fight, he was full of scars and had half-an-ear. Next door to Cliff's the Seeley's had one of those wire-haired terriers, and all it ever did was yap. My friend David had a cocker spaniel named Blackie. The dog was black as you might have guessed. Blackie was so smart that you couldn't even spell W-A-L-K around him before he'd go nuts. He loved his walks.

The Glenside Kid

A couple houses down from us lived my friend Carolyn and her mother and step father who was a retired English military officer. They had a wire haired terrier, Binky, and also a cat. What made the story worth mentioning is that her step father was named Dick Whittington, I kid you not. **Dick Whittington and His Cat** is a British folk tale that has often been used as the basis for stage pantomimes and other adaptations. It tells of a poor boy in the 14th century who becomes a wealthy merchant and eventually the Lord Mayor of London because of the ratting abilities of his cat. The character of the boy is named after a real-life person, Richard Whittington, but the real Whittington did not come from a poor family and there is no evidence that he had a cat. You can't make stuff like this up.

The parrot bugs Mrs. Renninger

At the middle of the block – across the street from us - in one of the few houses where people seemed to come and go, came a married couple who, as it turns out, had a parrot. Each day in the summer they'd put the parrot's cage on the front porch where it would enjoy the fresh air. Almost directly across the street lived the Renninger's. The had a daughter, Carol, who was a few years younger than me, but still part of the crew. Each day at noon that summer Mrs. Renninger would call her daughter home for lunch.

She'd call "Carol" a few times and Carol would go home for lunch.

Now Mrs. Renninger didn't know about the parrot, but the parrot soon took the cue from her daily heralding and soon Mrs. "R" would call "Carol" and seconds later so would the parrot. This went on for about a week and Carol's mother got angrier and angrier. I heard her tell my mother, "There's some kid mocking me every day when I call Carol for lunch, and if I ever catch them they will be sorry."

Well Mom figured out that the "kid" was the parrot and soon Mrs. "R" was about the only one on the block not in on the gag. In fact it got to be so much fun that her accusation became a self fulfilling prophecy and each day she'd call "Carol", then so would the parrot, and then so would Richard, Jimmy, John, me…well you get the idea.

Finally she figured it out and probably felt like a fool. Hoodwinked by a feathered heckler.

Aunt Clare and Uncle Charlie had another Boston Terrier before Cookie and her name was Mitsy. When I was very young they told me they were taking her to the doggie doctor. I went along and was terribly disappointed when the doggie doctor turned out to be a human being. I was thinking it was going to be a doggie. What did I know?

They also had a brown-and-white hunting dog named Missy. The dog lived in a kennel behind their garage, never got in their house unless it was bitter cold. She was strictly an outdoor dog and a hunter except when it thundered, and then she was a big baby. For some reason every thunder storm brought Missy to our house. She'd leap the kennel fence and dash down the street and start pawing at our front door. We'd let her in, she'd run under the dining room table and hide there until the storm passed. I would then stick a leash on her and return her to the kennel. I figured that Cookie must have told her about us.

She, too, was a nice dog.

The Glenside Kid

Chapter XXXV – The Taylor kids were not caught up in sports

When the babies were born I told Colleen that I really hope one of them becomes an athlete – and she suggested that Lily might be the one, not Brett II. Why? I have no idea, but that was what she thought.

Because I was so active in sports – as a kid, and as an adult - I suspect that is why my own kids were never big on participation in organized athletics. Yet, today, my sons do like sports a lot and Brett is a zealous Flyers hockey fan.

Chris, the oldest, played midget football for the Willow Grove Boys Club and was a bat boy for the Ursinus College team I coached and, later, for the East Abington team I led.

Brett was never in to football or baseball, but acquitted himself well as a soccer player for the local Hunter Soccer Club – he was leading scorer in his age class one season – and later in junior high. A falling out with his junior high coach prompted an early retirement from the sport for him.

Chris and I golfed regularly for a couple of years – every Sunday morning – and he got to be a decent player. Brett golfed a couple of times and disliked it. My golf clubs are in the trunk of the Ford Taurus but haven't met a golf ball in earnest for close to a year. Chris, as I recall, retired from the sport a few years ago.

But since I grew up with few other spare time options, sports were always a huge part of my life. I have grown up with two chipped front teeth – acquired when I was in junior high, running unimpeded for a touchdown, when the kid in front of me, my blocker, turned to see where I was. Where I was, was right behind him and I ran in to his helmet with my face. We had no face guards in those days, in fact I was wearing a leather helmet. I coughed up pieces of teeth, lots of blood and, oh yes, the ball. I was three yards from scoring touchdown.

The Glenside Kid

Baseball was always my favorite sport. In my mind I was always much better than I really was.

Chapter XXXVI- The Kid gets a dose of reality

On the school playground I was a very good baseball player. In our choose-up games on the field across Easton Road from Glenside School I was always one of the captains. I got to choose my players. All summer long we'd play from morning to night. Kids would come and go, the games went on.

There were a load of us kids who loved baseball and made the games fun. There was Chippy O'Liver (the Irish kid, his real name was Oliver, but O'Liver suited us better), Jackie Heller, Joe Whipple, Donnie Kirkland, Snavely O'Malley and the usual suspects from my Oak Road neighborhood – Jimmy, John, Chuck, Albert, and David. Carolyn, the lone girl, was among the best players. Sometimes she was the other captain.

Hum it in there baby!

I had a *Ted Williams* model bat that I could really whip around. I could flat out hit. When the bat broke, as wooden bats inevitably do, I was never able to replicate it or the skills it brought to my game. Confidence? Of course.

I always had some very good equipment because my neighbor Dick Refsnyder saw to that. In fact Dick kept me in not only baseballs and bats, but also in caps and, occasionally, an almost worn out uniform. I always looked good.

For the choose-up games, our equipment consisted of whatever we could get. Wooden bats never died. If they cracked you pounded some nails in to them, wrapped them with black tire tape and you were back in action. In those days you could go to the Glenside Hardware store or Dimmers Sporting Goods and get a bat for a few bucks. The other day I saw an ad in the paper that listed bats starting at $149 and going all the way to $249. No one in my neighborhood could have afforded a bat at those prices. We'd have probably ended up playing soccer.

If a kid had a baseball or a bat he brought it, if not he just brought himself and a glove. It seemed like every kid had a glove. Actually I had three. One was a fielder's mitt, another was something called a Trapper's Mitt that I used when I played first base and, somewhere along the line, I came up with an old Catcher's mitt that we kids used when we played a two man game called "Balls and Strikes". Baseballs? Well, we loved new ones but seldom got to play with them, if we did have one we'd usually save it for a while and use it for catches.

At the 5&10 you could get something they called a "Nickel Rocket". It cost five cents, of course, and was sort of a baseball as in it was the size of one, was white and had red stitches, but that's about where the similarity ended. It was not leather. The cover was some kind of oil cloth or something equally slick. The stitches were red but not cotton, like a real baseball, but a few good whacks with a bat and they started to unravel.

Things went better when you had a real baseball. And we would play with one that had a horsehide cover until, literally, the cover fell off. When that happened, we took out the black tire tape and replaced the cover of the ball with it. Amazingly, though the tire tape was initially kind of sticky, the ball was still pretty lively without its' original cover.

The Glenside Kid

The only major league ball I ever got in my life I got at Shibe Park there with my mother for an A's-Senators day game. There were less than a thousand people in the stands, it was probably 1953. I shagged a foul ball and then took it home – and we played with it relentlessly until the cover fell off. I wish I had saved that ball.

But earlier than that, at the age of eleven organized baseball beckoned.

"You should be playing for the Glenside Midgets"

A kid from my school, Johnny Dark, played in one of our regular pick-up games in early spring and said, "You should be playing for the Glenside Midgets, you'd be a sure thing." I had thought about it then, I was ten and ten was the earliest age you could join and I didn't think I was ready so I waited a year.

On the first Saturday in April 1952 I went to the Glenside War Memorial and "signed up" with Coach Mike Legrande. He seemed to have it all under control, always called the bats, balls, bases, catcher's gear "stuff". "Go get the catcher's stuff," he'd yell and someone did.

I mention catcher because, though I never played the position, my friend Bobby Wambold convinced me that the quickest, surest way to make the team was as a catcher. Sounded reasonable to me so I told Coach Legrande that I wanted to be a catcher.

They don't call catcher's gear "The tools of ignorance" for no reason. I quickly learned that you didn't have to be nuts to be a catcher, but it surely would have been helpful.

I caught an intra-squad game that first day and by the end of it every knuckle on my right hand was bleeding. I pounded the mitt before every pitch, chanted what I heard Bob say, he was catching for the other team, "Humm it in here baby, let it fly" and the pitcher

The Glenside Kid

would throw it and if the batter swung I'd close my eyes and pray he didn't hit me on the head with his bat or, worse yet, foul one off of me.

I caught two more intra-squad games in practice over the next couple of weeks and, to be honest, I could see that Yogi Berra had nothing to fear from me. I was just short of dreadful, not only that but I hated it. But Coach Legrande kept putting me in there; probably because Wambold and I were the only two kids dumb enough to want to be catchers.

We played the dreaded Ardsley Reds in an exhibition game. Wambold started, I came in the game mid-way. I was excited, and I was awful. Every kid who got on base stole on me. Once I managed to throw my pickoff attempt over the centerfielder's head and the kid scored from first base. I was dropping third strikes, I was missing pitches. I had an idea what hell must be like.

After a couple of innings of sheer horror I told Coach Legrande that I didn't see myself as a catcher. He gave me no argument and put in some other poor soul to finish the game. My days as a catcher were over.

I still figured I was a lock to make the club because in every game I played I got a hit or two. I saw the ball well and could plunk liners over the infield with relative ease. They stuck me in the outfield and, from time-to-time, at second base. In the outfield you could almost take a nap, no one was ripping the cover off the ball. I liked playing second because there was a lot of action.

And then, as the season approached, all of a sudden a group of six or eight kids showed up one night at practice. I didn't know who they were. I was not the only kid on the team beginning to feel uneasy. They were all kids from a nearby private school – with rich sounding names, Woody this, Clay that, Warren something else. It was ominous. They were dreaded rich kids with expensive equipment and the look of private school all over them.

The Glenside Kid

My pal Johnny Dark said that they were friends of the assistant coach's kid, Henny Morris, who went to Chestnut Hill Academy. It turned out that the team they were going to play for over in Chestnut Hill had folded. All of a sudden we had a numbers problem on the Glenside Midgets and these kids didn't even live in Glenside. It wasn't fair, but adults often disregard fair in the interest of winning ballgames.

It was Saturday morning and the last practice game was scheduled before the season began and it was also the day the uniforms were to be given out. They had just twenty to give. The uniforms consisted of a black cap with a white "G", Glenside in script across the front in black, black sox. Pretty sharp I thought. I could picture me in one of them.

The Coach called us all together and said, quite bluntly, that we now had a numbers problem and some kids would have to be cut. I don't think a kid had ever been cut before in the history of the Glenside Midgets. But now - thanks to the interlopers from Chestnut Hill Academy – we had close to 30 in the mix. Several of us among the newcomers were nervous. The Coach said to practice hard that day and he'd give out the uniforms after the practice game.

We played a team from West Oak Lane. I didn't start, but did get in the game. I pinch-hit and smoked a double between two outfielders and felt like that hit should make me a lock for one of the uni's. In the bottom of that inning I dropped a fly ball in left field and allowed two runs to score. Oh, oh. The "lock" wasn't as secure as I thought.

We rallied and won the game in the bottom of the seventh – that's all the innings we ever played – and Coach Legrande called us all together.

He made the usual speech about how hard it was for him to choose the team – the same speech I myself made several times, later in life, as a college baseball coach – and then he started calling names. Dark got the nod, Wambold made it too. The eight private schoolers all were included – and then, slowly, he started on the last ten. It got to number 19 and I was still standing on the outside looking in. Another name, not mine, got called. It was #20 or nothing for me.

Coach Legrande looked me dead in the eye and I figured I had made it and then I noticed that Harry Dark, Johnny's ten-year-old brother, was standing next to me crying like a baby – and as he blubbered away the Coach called his name, not mine. Harry couldn't hit the broadside of a barn with a cannon but their father was one of Coach Legrande's assistants.

Politics, favoritism, call it what you like. I was the better player and I got screwed. I knew I was better than at least four of the private school kids and certainly better than Harry. But Harry's tears got him a uniform. Like winning the booby prize Coach Legrande said they'd be forming a B team and I was going to play for that club. The uniform for that club was cap (without even a letter) and white tee shirt with Glenside stenciled on it.

I told them that B team wasn't in my plans and handed back the hat and tee shirt. I hopped on my bike and rode home. Harry wasn't the only kid who shed tears that Saturday. I learned a lesson that day. The following year I made the club – and then played Junior League ball for the North Penn VFW Post 676 team after that, but I never forgot that I was initially cut because some other kid shed some tears and had a better insider connection than me.

The biggest game I ever played

Perhaps the biggest, most important, game I ever played in wasn't organized ball at all – except by the kids in my neighborhood.

It was the summer of 1953 and we were playing a pickup game on the field across from Glenside School – and it was a rollicking good one. Lots of kids, pretty close to 18 of us, actually. Every summer day was pretty much like that. A game, kids coming

The Glenside Kid

and going. And then a couple of kids from the Keswick/Abington section of town appeared and, basically, challenged us to a game for Glenside's "bragging rights".

"We'll kick your butts," said their ring-leader, a kid named Billy Delanzo. The other kid was Charlie Buzzard, a onetime friend of Richard Cliff. Blizzard was a blond-haired, arrogant, fat kid. I never liked him and I saw no indication that the situation was going to change anytime soon.

Since I was the leader of our pick-up games I agreed to the contest and then stated the terms. It would be on our field and we'd try to recruit unbiased umps – older kids, or grown ups if we could. No one over 14 could play. And they agreed to it all. Some of my friends were worried, "They'll stack their team with ringers," Snavely said.

I went to my neighbor, Mr. Refsnyder, and told him about the game and asked if we could borrow some equipment – and he said, "sure, what do you need?" He provided a set of catcher's gear (Bobby Wambold was gonna play, he just didn't know it yet), some bats, a bag of slightly used baseballs, three bases and an old, kind of worn out looking, home plate.

John Ewing's father, Don, said he'd umpire. That was really good and he also offered to help us get the field ready. I always liked Mr. E, Tommy King from across the street said he'd also umpire.

The game was set for Saturday at noon and we worked the whole day before getting the field ready. Several of us brought push lawn mowers to the field, somebody got a hold of a bag of lime to line the bases. When we were finished, the field looked pretty sharp. We didn't have uniforms but Mr. Refsnyder gave me a box of two dozen baseball caps – blue cap, red brim. We'd all having matching heads anyway.

The Glenside Kid

As expected Delanzo and Buzzard showed up with a motley looking crew of kids. A few looked like thugs, some older than 14 for sure, but hey a game was a game and, thankfully, Mr. Ewing took charge. He was tall, athletic looking and his graying hair was always worn in a crew cut. For the occasion he actually dressed in blue. No one would be crazy enough to challenge him. Mr. Refsnyder showed up and umped the bases. Tommy was a no show.

Our team had Wambold behind the plate, my close friend Chuck Danihel on first, Jackie Heller on second, Carolyn Scott (yes a girl) at shortstop and Chip Oliver on third. Joe Wiedler was in left, Janie Masters (another girl) was in center and Donnie Kirkland was in right. John, Jimmy Hager, Snavely O'Malley, Dave Hurlock, Rich Masters and Dave Morin formed our bench. The girls, Scott and Masters, may have been the best athletes on the field – and when the Delanzo/Buzzard team made fun of our using two girls I just chuckled. (Later in life they were both college All-American field hockey players, later scholastic coaches.)

I took the mound and mowed down the opponents easily for the first four frames. Why hadn't I tried out as a pitcher for the midgets? Confidence – or lack of it, I guess. Their pitcher Patrick Slater did the same to us for the first three. Slater, by the way, was a bit of a thug, but a terrific pitcher.

And then in the bottom of the fourth Carolyn led off with a single, Heller followed with a double and then I drove them both in with a sharp hit to right. Danihel hit a shot to dead center over the fielder's head and I scored. We were up 3-0.

In the fifth a big kid for the "Buzzards" named Nick Spencer rocked one of my pitches over Janie's head and circled the bases. It was 3-1. Buzzard got a hit, and then Slater followed. Delanzo hit a screaming liner to Oliver at third, it came so hard it almost knocked him over, but he looked in his glove and, by God, he caught it and doubled up Slater.

The Glenside Kid

In the bottom of the inning we added three more runs when Danihel parked one over the left fielder's head with the bases loaded. He wasn't the fastest human being ever and just managed a triple, not a homer. It was 6-1.

They closed the gap to 6-3 in the top of the sixth and the inning ended with the bases loaded when one of their stalwarts hit a feeble pop up to Oliver at third. Chippy was in the right spot again. We didn't score in the bottom of the frame. But I was tired and I felt like my arm was going to fall off, I had never pitched in a game like this and so, as player-manager, I summoned Carolyn to the mound. The Buzzards, of course, hooted and started licking their chops. "A girl," one crowed, "the game is ours."

But their initial catcalls quickly went silent when she struck out the first two batters – both looking, and Mr. Ewing emphatically rung them up. The third one hit a weak fly to John Ewing now stationed in right. The inning was over.

The game should have ended after seven – kid sandlot games never went longer than that, but Delanzo wanted to keep playing. Figuring, maybe, they'd get to the girl in the next inning. I took a poll of my team – we were up by three runs – and they said they'd play nine. Mr. Ewing and Mr. Refsnyder were also okay with it.

So we batted in the bottom of the seventh and added two insurance runs. We were now up 8-3 and the opponents were really getting quiet.

Carolyn gave up hits to the first two batters in the top of the eighth and looked over at me, now playing shortstop, and said, "I don't think I can finish this." I walked to the mound and said, "What would you do?" She said "Let Janie pitch". And that's what I did. Carolyn jogged out to center and Janie got the next three hitters in order. No cat calls this time about a girl pitching. Two of them had quieted the Buzzards.

In the bottom of the eighth we batted around, scoring five more runs. It was 13-3 when the ninth began and Mr. Ewing actually asked Delanzo if they wanted to continue playing – they were down ten runs. They said that they did.

Chippy Oliver took the mound for us in the ninth and, though he gave up a run and two hits, the outcome of the game was never in doubt. We were all tired, but we won 13-4 and owned bragging rights for all of Glenside sandlots for the year. It was as good as it got.

Chapter XXXVII – Doing stuff with the kids

As we visited the twins, almost weekly, I would sit and tell little Brett about all the things we were going to do as he got older. I doubt he knew what I was talking about, but it made me feel good. Doing stuff is important and, as the twins' parents will soon learn, they are little for such a short time.

One of the things that we did with our kids was make sure they had a nice vacation trip someplace each summer. A few times it was Cape Cod – which the grown-ups liked better than the kids did and, finally, our annual trip to the South Jersey shore.

We made sure that each seashore vacation also included a fishing trip. While the kids didn't always like putting the bait on the hooks, they did like the boat ride and, occasionally, they'd catch something. Once Brett nailed a huge flounder and still talks about it to this day.

We'd use minnows sometimes and, as I recall it, both Brett and Melissa, when little, wanted to bring the minnows home as pets – and sometimes we actually did. Minnows look like gold fish, except they appear to be green.

Squid was also a favorite bait. People eat it too. I prefer it as bait.

When I was a kid going fishing was a cool thing to do mostly because I got to do it with my step father and his pals. I hope that, one day, Brett, Little Brett, maybe Uncle Chris and I can go fishing together.

Chapter XXXVIII - Gone Fishing with Ernie

It's March 5, 1955 and Ernie officially becomes my step father. Here he and Mom cut the wedding cake in our dining room.

My step-father, Ernie, was a man's man. He liked it all, sports, politics, current events, reading about the Civil War. But among the things he liked the best was going fishing. I was luke warm about the sport but not about being with him and whatever he was doing. So if he said "Let's go fishing", I said, "Ready when you are Pop."

It's 4.30 AM, a Wednesday in June as I recall, and Ernie yanked me out of my nice, snug, bed. We were going fishing out of Avalon, NJ and it was a good two hour drive to get there,

We put away a cup of coffee, munched on a piece of toast while awaiting the arrival of Dad's work buddies – Joe Bates and Matt Repinski. Joe was a short, muscular Italian guy (Bates, obviously was the Anglicized version of some longer Italian name) and Matt was a big, muscular guy. I assumed he was Polish. Ernie always called him a "Polack" preceded, usually, by the words "Big, dumb..."

The Glenside Kid

They arrived, we climbed aboard Joe's vintage Hudson, and we were off for a day of male bonding. This was truly guy stuff. Life gets no better. Mom and my sister were sound asleep upstairs. I doubt they even knew we left.

The sun makes funny designs on the South Jersey sky as it comes up and you are motoring down Route 73 to the coast to pursue the adventure of catching fish. The sky this day had many colors and seemed to suggest that getting up early would be well worth the trip.

I was just a teenager but with these three guys I felt ten feet tall. We talked about the Phillies, what good night Olney's Del Ennis had just had against the Cincinnati Reds. We couldn't imagine why they weren't winning with great players like Granny Hamner, Richie Ashburn, Stan Lopata and Curt Simmons.

The miles drifted by. We stopped at a worn out looking chrome diner and had another cup of coffee. Time was fleeting.

Joe was driving and his two-tone maroon car was old and rattled over every bump in the road. I hoped it would make it. And, finally, we did. Right off the main drag in to Avalon, just over the Ocean Drive Bridge, was a sandy, rutted road that took us down toward the fishing place, nestled against the bay.

We pulled in to the parking lot – it was pebbles and crushed clam shells – both of which made pinging sounds as we drove over them. Joe slid the Hudson right up next to the building. An old, weather beaten and quite faded, Coca Cola signed proclaimed this to be "Jim's Place".

We went to the trunk and pulled out our fishing gear. It was my first chance to use the new Ocean City reel that Ernie had given me for Christmas – and it fit right on my long, green, fiber glass fishing rod. It was just about 7 AM.

The Glenside Kid

We entered Jim's. The wooden screen door slammed behind us – Ka-bamm – and the noise perked up a character behind the counter that I knew had to be Jim.

He was tanned, in fact his skin looked like a leathery old saddle. His black hair was thinning and touched with gray. He was tall – reedy would be an apt description – and he looked like he was supposed to look, clear blue eyes, stubble of a beard and a few teeth short of the number he was supposed to have. Isn't it amazing, I thought, God always seems to cast people in exactly the right roles.

Jim gave us the usual pitch about how we should have been here last week when you had to, literally, beat off the fish so as you wouldn't catch too many and sink your boat.

Ernie, who had been frequenting Jim's for years, laughed and reminded him that his name really should be Chuck – as in "Chuck full of shit". I laughed, this was all part of the ritual. A ritual that I was in awe of. Man, life was sure good.

Finally we headed toward our boat. We had our minnows, our squid and all sorts of chum needed for fishing – and four hoagies bought at Rizzo's the day before, plenty of beer for the men, sodas for me. The boat was called a Garvey. This particular boat appeared to have last been painted sometime before the Great Depression, it had a small cabin and some weather beaten benches around the sides and rear. It reeked of seaweed and long dead fish scales. They explained to me that it had a flat bottom and was best used to fish in, what they called, "The Paddies". I had no idea what that was. Joe seemed to prefer fishing in them.

The paddies looked like the swamps to me, but Joe assured me that they were primo fishing grounds. And once there they fished, drank beer, told really terrible grown-up jokes ate the hoagies and then drank some more beer.

Dad called Joe a "cowboy" because he always fished with two poles. One day he cast both lines out, put them down in the buckles (on the side of the boat) and reached for a beer. At that precise moment two denizens of the paddies struck – one per pole – and both his rods disappeared off the boat. They were gone forever. Joe was not a happy man, but he compensated by drinking more beer.

The day, the bait, the hoagies and the beers go quickly when you are having a good time and this day went by fast too. We came in at the end of it, dragged our fishing gear, a bucket of fish we caught, and loaded it all in the trunk. We were tired, but a good and self satisfying tired. And the trip home seemed to take less time than the one down.

The downside of trips such as this was, always, that you had to clean the fish. Ernie knew how and I learned. I disliked this chore immensely. Mom wanted no parts of fish heads.

Gone, though the times might be, as a wonderful memory it lives on as one of those times when a teenaged boy did some serious growing up in the company of some very good men.

Chapter XXXVIX – Junior High Days

My neighbor, Dr. Ernest Harting, always equated teaching at the junior high school level as being the equivalent of digging ditches. A lifelong educator and onetime principal of Temple University High School, he talked about the raging hormones that early teens experience as they try to decide what or who they will become.

When he heard that I wanted to become a teacher, he said, "Teach elementary school or high school, never become a junior high school teacher."

Most kids survive junior high. I did, so did my friends. In fact though it was but a three-year blip on the radar screen of life, it provided some nice memories for me. I can't vouch for the teacher's take on all this.

After seven years at Glenside School (including Kindergarten) and seven years of being a short walk from my yearly classroom, I now faced a daily trek up Limekiln Pike to the school bus stop on Waverly Road.

There were a bunch of us making that trip daily, so it was a social thing. We'd get up there and hope that the bus would be late, or better yet, a no show. Once in awhile that actually happened and then somebody's mother would take us and our late arrival was "excused". How cool was that?

The school district didn't own the buses, an outfit called "Duckloe Bus Company" had the contract and instead of yellow school buses they provided old Greyhound luxury buses. Norm Duckloe was usually our driver and he was a nice guy. I think Norm owned the company. If you had to ride a bus to school you might as well go in style.

Thomas Williams Junior High School was our destination it was located in Wyncote – one town over from Glenside - on Hewitt

Road and to it came kids from our school and two other township elementary schools – the elementary school students were actually whacked up evenly between TW and Elkins Park Junior.

Dr. Edward Worthington was the principal, but the real power there was Miss Stauffer who was technically the "guidance counselor" but she was calling the shots.

Since my name was at the end of the alphabet I got in a homeroom where kids whose last names began with R and beyond were housed. Our homeroom teacher was John Weaver. Mr. Weaver was also destined to be my shop teacher. Friends like Jerry Stremic and Larry Strange, from Glenside School, were in my homeroom. So was a kid named Johnny Wyrostek, whose father played for the Phillies, and Carolyn Walters, whose Dad was a former star player and now a coach for the Milwaukee Braves. I could always find a baseball connection.

Thomas Williams Junior High, I loved the place

I can honestly say that I loved junior high school. What did Dr. Harting know? It was a growing up experience and being with older kids was a positive change for me. I was sick of the little pesky elementary school kids.

The Glenside Kid

The toughest teacher I've ever had in my life, Elsie Acker, taught math at TW and it's a miracle I survived. It's why I teach English today and not math. I grew to hate math. Hamilton Lampe, or English teacher, inspired me. He introduced me to books that brought the word to life – and he convinced me that I could be a writer. The phys ed teacher was named Coach Frey (later I found out that he had a real first name, Paul) and Phil Finkeldey was our football coach and he also taught history.

We had a Spanish teacher named Mrs. Helen Dobrynin. She was a tough cookie and my pals and I liked her a lot. She was always up for a joke and if you messed around in class she had no compunction about throwing the first thing she could lay her hands on at you.

One day my friends Jerry Stremic, Larry Strange and I decided we'd put a thumb tack on her chair. So we got there early and placed the tack dead center.

She sauntered in to class and, while we held our breath, she finally sat at her desk – and never flinched. "Did the tack fall off," I wondered and I looked at Jerry and Larry. They were equally puzzled.

The class ended when the bell sounded and as we got up to leave she said, "Taylor, Stremic and Strange, stay behind, I want to speak with you". We knew that we were toast.

"I know what you guys did," she said, "And I didn't want to give you the satisfaction of it." She sat on the tack all class long. "Just remember," she said, "Payback is a bitch". She was okay in our books and never did exert the "pay back", though we worried about it all year.

In seventh grade Mr. Fink coached the JV football team and I won my first athletic letter. We won all our games but one, losing to the roughnecks from Ambler Junior High by a lopsided score. The letter I won was a linked "TW" and I needed a sweater for it.

The Glenside Kid

Mom decided to get me one for Christmas – and she initially failed. My Mom never failed.

TW's colors were black and orange and she soon learned that nobody made that combination letterman's sweater. After turning the city upside down she settled for a black sweater with yellow stripes (it was intended for Lincoln High) and then she sewed orange ribbon over the yellow. If nothing else, she was resourceful.

It was in one of Coach Frey's gym classes that I discovered that I really hated gymnastics and he required that we take part in rope climbing, spring board jumping and all that nonsense. Hey Coach, let us play basketball and be done with it will ya? Mostly, he did. But when we got to the gym for phys ed and saw the mats off the wall and on the floor we all got that sick feeling.

The gym was also used for occasional lunch time "sock hops". And that meant you had to take off your shoes and, literally, dance in your stocking feet. Lots of kids wore cleats – or taps – on their shoes in those days and the "socks only" rule was done to preserve the floor's finish.

We conducted paper drives at TW, scavenging newspapers from all over creation. As a member of student council I got to be one of the big honchos and on paper drive day I didn't ever go to class, instead I'd supervise the dropping off and re-loading of the newspapers in to a big truck.

When I made the varsity football team in eighth grade I had one of those moments when you wish you could disappear. It was raining hard but it was decided that we were going to play. Coach Fink ordered "mud cleats" for our shoes. These cleats are much longer than the usual ones so that your shoes would really dig in to the turf. Well I put mine on, leaped up from the bench and flew up in the air, landing flat on my back. The laughter was deafening.

Another thing that almost sunk me at TW was Industrial Arts (or "shop" as we called it). To pass the class you had to use a jig saw and cut out the school emblem and mount it on a wooden plaque. T and W has lots of cuts and I busted one after another. Things were getting desperate when one of the kids, Eddie Capreri I think, told me he'd cut a TW out for me. And he did. I passed.

When I was in ninth grade a notice was posted that Overbrook High School from Philadelphia – and their star player Wilt "The Stilt" Chamberlain – would be playing a scrimmage game at Cheltenham High. If you wanted to go there'd be a bus to take you. A lot of us went and there we saw the largest human being we'd even seen. Chamberlain topped seven feet tall and was an incredible player.

When Wilt first ran out on the court for warm ups he wore a cap and a white scarf around his neck. He was a show-off and had the talent to back it up. They slaughtered Cheltenham by the way.

The Glenside Kid

Chapter XL – I help close the park

When our kids were teenagers we lived on Susquehanna Road in Abington and right across the street were our friends, the Simpson's – Jack, Joanne and their kids.

Jack was an Abington cop and talked me in to joining the township's volunteer "Special Police" unit. I always liked the idea of law enforcement and so I joined.

We were not "Rent-a-cops" but citizen police. I likened it to being in the National Guard. We were sworn officers of the law, dressed in complete police uniforms and got all kinds of training, including firearms – though they didn't want us to be armed on duty. (As an aside, most of us usually did arm ourselves figuring that if we were out in public dressed as police the bad guys wouldn't bother to make the distinction.)

While a lot of what we did was volunteer work – church crossings, weather emergencies, football game traffic patrols and the like - every so often some paid duty came along and we happily took that. A buck is a buck.

Once there was a trash strike – all the trash men walked off the job and trash was piling up everywhere. Finally both Abington and Cheltenham Townships decided to hire outside contractors to collect the trash and garbage and that meant that the unions would be unhappy and that things could get ugly. The special police got mobilized.

I road in an Abington Police car with Sgt. Bob Kerstetter and one block from the station house Bob pulled the car over, popped the trunk, and directed me to go get the shotgun. I did as told and it sat on my lap as we approached Cheltenham's Wall Park where a major confrontation was anticipated.

To make matters worse, the Rev. Ralph Abernathy showed up on behalf of the strikers. And while it may have been lost on the workers, the Rev and his associates arrived in a limousine and he was wearing denim work clothes, albeit professionally tailored. He made a speech, they cheered. The other trash men showed up and, ringed by police, yours truly included, picked up the festering waste materials and left.

I was never so glad to see trash picked up in my life and nothing happened.

But a couple of years later we got another paid job that made me nostalgic for my childhood. Captain Bill Slade, our leader, struck a deal with the owners of Willow Grove Park that we would be on patrol there, to augment their rent-a-cops, on closing day (forever) of the park.

The owners expected problems and they thought a show of force might head it off. And to be honest it did.

We were all told to be visibly armed that day, I was wearing a 38 with a six inch barrel and beautiful bone grips. One park visitor commented on the piece and said, "Look what the 'man' is carrying, I wouldn't want to mess with that gun." Point well taken. He wouldn't.

Chapter XLI - "Life was a lark", so said the ad

I've already established what a great place Glenside was to grow up in, but another of its assets was the close proximity to Willow Grove Park where, as the ads said on radio, TV and in the newspapers, "Life is a lark".

As kids we spent a lot of our summer free time haunting the huge amusement park right off Easton Road in Willow Grove (actually in Abington Township as it turned out, but who knew…or for that matter even cared).

Our monetary goal for such trips was scraping enough money together for a trolley car ride from the stop at Royal Avenue to the terminal at the Welsh Road end of the park. The park, of course, was originally created by the Philadelphia transit authority as a way for people to spend money on trolley rides, back at the turn of the 20th Century. I think the round trip might have been 30-cents.

Once we got to the park we 'spent" our Supplee-Sealtest tickets that we gathered all summer long by purchasing ice cream, popsicles and the like at local food stores. Every kid had long strips of these tickets that earned you a free ride – or one at greatly reduced prices - on just about every thing. The Terminal Diner is still there and, as a kid, we often grabbed a hot dog and a soda there when we got off the trolley and before we walked through the tunnel under Easton Road and entered the park.

When I was smaller it was a place to go with the neighborhood kids – Jimmy, John, Richard, Karen. When I grew older it was a great place to go on a date because girls would squeal and snuggle closer, especially on the roller coasters.

There were three roller coasters at Willow Grove Park. The most scary was called "The Thunderbolt" and it seemed that at least once-a-summer some young guy (often a sailor from the local Naval Air Station base) would fall out and get killed. There was also "The Alps" which had a brakeman and a lot of Plaster-of-Paris shaped mountain sides to ride through. It was a decent date vehicle, though. My favorite was called "The Scenic", though some called it "The Baby Scenic". It ran free, no brakeman, but was short ride right over the picnic groves.

Other key attractions were the "Tunnel of Love" – also a great place to take a date because it was (a.) slow and (b.) dark and (c.) the water was quite shallow so even if the boat sunk you weren't going to drown. The "Fun House" usually wasn't much fun for me. I dislike being scared, so I generally avoided it. It also made some vulgar noises.

That's the Alps in the lower right hand corner of this aerial shot of the park, The Thunderbolt is in the upper left.

"The Whip" was fun and sooner or later someone would inevitably lose their lunch on it. There were air ships that were pretty tame and a wide variety of mid-way games where you could impress young ladies with your marksmanship or your ability to knock down milk bottles and win her a kewpie doll.

A large lake had both pedal boats (fun on a date) and a huge Swan that chugged around (not as much fun). There was at least one very cool merry-go-round with carved horses.

The Glenside Kid

Lots of food could be had – likely none of it actually nourishing – and you always had to be on the look-out for a seedier, city, element that would come to the park looking for trouble. This became more and more the case as the park aged and maintenance seemed like an idea management never understood.

While other similar parks have thrived nationally, Willow Grove Park fell in to disrepair and, eventually, closed. The World's largest bowling alley was built there and lasted a few years. Why did it perish? Well the lanes all warped because some genius decided it was okay to build it over a spot that was known for its springs. Yes, Willow Grove once also housed "The Mineral Springs Hotel", a resort where people came for healthful mineral spring's baths.

When the park finally closed it became the site of a huge shopping mall, called, of all things, "The Willow Grove Park Mall". They even put in a merry-go-round. But the heritage of the amusement park is gone, lost, I'm afraid forever, much like our youth.

Chapter XLII – Not Irish Twins

Our son Brett and daughter Melissa are considered Irish twins.

The term is used to describe two children born to the same mother in the same calendar year or within twelve months of each other. The phrase originated as a derogatory term associated with Irish immigration to the United States and England in the 1800's. The implication was that large groups of close-in-age siblings were the result of uneducated, poor Irish Catholic families' lack of birth control as well as self-control.

In modern use, the term is not intended as an insult, but rather a description of siblings born close together. Irish twins are not actually twins and they are not the same as having twins, which are defined as two siblings born from the same gestation.

Brett was born April 10, 1969 and Melissa show up on April 6, 1970. Each year, for four days, they are the same age. As far as I know they like the designation.

They have been exceedingly close for their wholes lives, just as if they were real twins.

I had a sister, too. She is three years younger than me – and she didn't become my sister until I was 15. Having a sister was a nice thing, I thought that then. I still do.

But the babies, Brett II and Lily are real twins and as such will have a lifetime together of close friends, shared experiences and a loving family.

The Glenside Kid

Chapter XLIII - Waking up my sister

I didn't have a sister until I was 15. My sister, Pat, was originally my cousin Pat. In fact as a result of my Mom marrying my Uncle Ernie I was also my own cousin, my Mom was her own sister-in –law and so on. It always makes for an amusing story.

Ernie was married to my Dad's sister, Florence Taylor. When she died a few years after my Dad did it seemed like fate ordained that he and Pat would join me and my mom and form a family. Since Taylor blood ran through both Pat and my veins we were more than just step brother and step sister. We were more like half-brother, half-sister.

Anyway when two families became one I got the dubious daily task of having to awaken my sister. I'd have rather faced the Black Devils gang.

That's my sister who is clearly amused about something, my Mom looks annoyed, Ernie is just drinking his coffee

Pat is a sweet person once she is awake, but an absolute terror when awakened from a sound sleep. She threatened to hurt you when you woke her up before she was ready and I believed that she was capable of such mayhem.

I always suspected that Pop didn't want to mess with her either and so he left the dirty job to me.

The day would begin when I'd be awakened by our Boston Terrier, Cookie. Mom would dispatch her up the steps to get me. "Go get Teddy," she'd command and the dog obeyed. She came flying up the steps, my bedroom was at the top of the stairs, took a leap at the doorway and landed on me. Then Cookie nuzzled me until I woke up, chasing me under the covers if necessary. But even the dog wouldn't mess with my sister.

I tried many different methods of waking her up and all they succeeded in doing was getting something thrown at me or, at the very least, me having to listen to some words not normally in the vocabulary of a 12 year-old-girl. She was no day in the park in the early morning.

Finally, like an inspiration from above, I hit upon a fool proof method. This was a sure-fire solution that would do the job and, at the same time, keep me out of harm's way.

In the far corner of her bedroom – she had the middle room of three on the second floor – stood an ancient 21-inch black-and-white Philco TV. It was about the size of a small boat. She liked that old TV despite the fact that most channels came in fuzzy (she had a poor rabbit ear's antenna) and some of the knobs had fallen off and gone to wherever it is old TV knobs go.

My solution was this. Each morning, after Cookie woke me, I'd tip toe in to her room, flick on the old TV, turn the volume as high as it would go and then tip toe out again.

Old Philco TV's took time to warm up – so that by the time hers came on I was already downstairs and protected by Mom and Dad at the breakfast table. That time lapse saved me before the blaring TV rooted her out of bed, shouting expletives as she went. The sounds coming from that room were enough to make grown men quake in fear. It worked though and because she was notoriously sluggish first thing in the morning I was out the door and on my way to school before she dressed and made it downstairs. The three year gap in our ages meant that we never actually were in the same school at the same time.

She got her revenge on a regular basis by waiting until I was taking a shower and then flushing the downstairs toilet. That usually scalded me. Or, at times, she'd run the hot water and I'd freeze to death. Nice kid, but I fully understood that pay back is a bear.

Plumbing in the older houses afforded such amenities to revenge-minded siblings. Newer homes are, of course, made better and TV's come on instantly. But neither are as much as we had with the older models, and they provided yet another ritual of growing up.

Chapter XLIV – Religion is still at the center of things

I am Presbyterian, my wife is Catholic. We were married by a district judge in Elkton, MD, not in a church. It seemed the best way to handle the situation at the time.

Our older two kids were raised in Carmel Presbyterian Church, the two younger ones at Our Lady Help of Christian's RC church.

We attend church, when we go, at Carmel. Usually at Easter, perhaps at Christmas, maybe another time or two. Do I miss it? Yes, because growing up church was an important part of my life. I have personally read the Bible from cover-to-cover twice. God and I have a nightly chat before I go to sleep.

Statistics tell us that a large majority of people skip church regularly but still consider themselves religious. We are in that majority, I'd say.

All of our kids, and grandkids, have been baptized in various churches – Carmel included. And now the twins will be baptized in a church near their home in North Wales because their parents believe that it is important.

What happened to religion? It has become the fodder for endless debate. Among the excuses, or reasons, is that people got too busy. At one time few worked on Sunday, now lots of people do. Or they work six days and sleep in on Sunday to get some rest.

Our legislators have pretty much managed to expunge a lot of the Christian faith from our daily lives. We used to say prayers in school – planned or the ones we uttered before a really important test – and that's taboo now. Sadly the Abington School District was once at the center of legal action to expel God from schools. Are we better off? I doubt it.

The Glenside Kid

The yearly assaults on Christmas decorations in public places – schools now have winter holidays, not Christmas vacations – and, just lately, a school district in Ohio expelled a traditional Easter Egg hunt from their vacation calendar, inserting instead a "Spring Egg Hunt" are nonsense and political correctness run amok.

Then there are also the nut jobs who find religion to be a handy excuse to kill people who don't agree with them. It's been going on for centuries, it never seems to change and I'm sure God is not pleased by all that nonsense.

I wish that children, especially, would get more exposure to religion. I think it teaches lessons of goodness and charity and understanding. As a youngster growing up in Glenside, church was a central part of my life. All my childhood friends went to church, too. Some went to the Methodist Church, some to the Lutheran, the Baptist or the Catholic Church – but we all went. Our Sunday plans always began with the words "After church we'll..." It's what you did in those days and it made you a better person.

In 2007 I helped with the PR for Carmel's 125th anniversary celebration and former members came from far and near to take part in that wonderful celebration..

Chapter XLIV – Christ taught my Sunday School class

When I was a teenager Christ was my Sunday school teacher at Carmel Presbyterian Church.

I got your attention didn't I?

Actually it was Jack Christ, not Jesus, but with a name like that a calling to religion is a natural. (The name was pronounced cryst and the family were longtime Carmel members.) Jack taught us – a small group of teenaged guys – in a small room off the choir loft. He was a cool guy – probably early 20's, really knew the Bible and he got the message across and we came every week to be with him.

I had lots of dedicated Sunday school teachers at Carmel – Jimmy Armstrong (a student minister), Dot Zeigenfuss and Willis Kesler to name a few. As a kid growing up in the 1940's and 50's church was a very important part of my life. It was the spiritual center of all we did, for sure, but it was also educational and, even more importantly, it was social.

My Mom's family was among the earliest members of Carmel Presbyterian Church. It is located at the intersection of Limekiln Pike and Mt. Carmel Avenue in the Abington part of Glenside. It is not and never was "Mount Carmel Presbyterian Church" though people have mistakenly called it that for over a century now.

The first church sanctuary was constructed in 1894-1995 and dedicated on January 26, 1896. The Roth family was part of that congregation. By 1924 church membership, including Mom and her seven siblings, had grown to 662 and the church school was 825. The old building was torn down and a new sanctuary started in the winter of 1924-25.

Carmel membership continued to grow as the surrounding communities were developed. The highest church membership reported for Carmel was 2256 in 1952 when I was a boy. The

The Glenside Kid

corresponding high figure for the church school was 1816 in 1949. It was determined that further building expansion was necessary. A new administration and church school building was constructed, dedicated on October 27, 1957. I was there for that.

Carmel Presbyterian Church

Dr. Howard J. Bell was the pastor when I was a small kid, he was a kindly, white haired man, but was soon replaced by his son the Rev. James Bell. The new minister was loved by the kids (like me) and we called him "Jimmy". The younger church members also related to Jimmy, who had joined the church right out of seminary as his father's assistant.

My mom once pointed out that the older folks in the church didn't like him because (a.) he wasn't his father and (b.) he was too young. Soon Jimmy fixed them all and left. It was a bleak day for us. He became the pastor of a new Presbyterian church in nearby Flourtown and a significant number of young Carmel members followed him there. Mom and I actually went for a few services there.

Jimmy was followed to the pulpit by another younger minister (we made an editorial decision here to not use his name).

The Glenside Kid

Again, the kids liked him and the younger ladies adored him. The Reverend was a handsome guy. Soon the older element decided that (a.) he was too good looking (I once heard an elderly church lady actually say that) and (b.) he didn't jump through hoops when told to. There was a pattern developing, and even as a kid I could see that a certain cadre of people ran the church with an iron fist.

It was mostly during Jimmy Bell's two immediate successors tenure at Carmel that I served as an usher – a prestigious thing for a teenager in those days. I was active in youth fellowship and played on both the basketball team and the softball teams. As I got to be an older teen I also experienced the church camp, Kirkwood, in the Poconos and learned that coeds from nearby Beaver College frequently attended services at the church and, a few times, actually did the Poconos thing too. Abington school district kids and Cheltenham school district kids, usually arch rivals, formed interesting alliances at the church.

There were always more teenaged guys who wanted to be ushers than they had room for. It was prestigious to be picked and your first year you kind of interned – you had to be 16. Once you got to be a veteran you then had the power over the other kids. The church ran three services every Sunday and we needed at least six or eight guys for each one. We even had officers. I was once the vice president. The neat part about ushering was that as soon as we marched up the aisle and collected the money we all split from the church – seldom heard the sermon, and walked down the hill to Kenyon's diner where I learned to enjoy a good cup of coffee.

The ushers also formed the nucleus of the sports teams that were key activities for the teens at the church. Inside the church was a basketball court, not so big but one we could access almost anytime and two bowling alleys. I figured we Presbyterians were pretty well rounded.

Carmel's sports teams were good and we always competed for championships in leagues sponsored, usually, by the Abington YMCA. In fact it was in 1957 that I played on the only undefeated

The Glenside Kid

team of my life, the basketball team that went 14-0 against squads like Salem Baptist, Glenside Methodist and St. Paul's Lutheran.

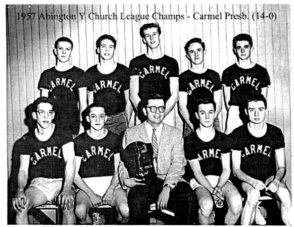

The Glenside kid is at end of row, top right – we were 14-0

I taught a Sunday School class when I was freshman education major in college. Since I was home almost every weekend anyway, my mom suggested to the head honcho at the church school that I'd be a likely candidate to teach a class of kids – we were thinking elementary school age. What they gave me was a class of ten high school girls – some of whom were stunners and only a year or two younger than me – and my weekly dilemma was whether to teach them or flirt with them. Soon my girlfriend learned of my exposure to ten potential rivals every Sunday and decided I should end that phase of my teaching career – and I did.

Speaking of Sunday School, every year they had something outdoors, usually in the spring, called "Rally Day" at which time you earned your attendance badge for the year. Since I was almost always there, I had a string of those attendance bars that made me look like a general when I wore them on the lapel of my jacket. Yes, we dressed up for church in those days – coat, tie, white shirt. That attire showed respect for the Lord and for the church. I couldn't imagine it any other way. I still wear a coat and tie when I attend. They also gave us bookmarker ribbons for the Bible that each person got when they became a church member. I still have my Bible, given to me when I became a church member, filled with those markers.

Two wonderful pastors inspired me as I got older. One was Dr. John A. Lampe and the other was Dr. James Eby. The current pastor is Dr. James Thornton, who seems to be an excellent fit and I enjoy his sermons.

Sadly it's not the same there – or at most churches - any more. There's plenty of blame to go around, I suppose. It's not that they don't try, because they try harder than ever. The older people who ran the church (most churches) with an iron fist for the latter half of the twentieth century finally got old and died. I could pick up the *Carmel Courier* church newsletter for decades and it was always the same people making the key decisions. For the longest time young people were not really encouraged to take a role, other than in the most passive or mundane ways. The older leaders often controlled things, believing that they were right, so much so that younger people grew disillusioned with them and, as a consequence, the church itself and either went elsewhere or simply gave up on organized religion all together. I consider myself both a Carmel member and a Christian, I still send regular donations to the church, but I don't attend as often as I should.

The decline in church attendance nationally is alarming. Some stats tell you that fifty years ago churches were filled with 80 per cent of their members every Sunday and now it's something less than 20 per cent. Some of it, I'm sure, also has to do with political correctness. The nut fringe attack Christmas regularly and the ACLU backs them up. You can find symbols of other faiths during the Christmas holidays, but not much to do with the actual observation of Christmas. Santa Claus, of course, has nothing to do with religion but even he frequently gets the bums rush from the ACLU. The Christmas season is not the "Winter Holidays"; at least it never will be in my mind. Holidays are Memorial Day, Labor Day and so on.

The Glenside Kid

This country was founded as a majority Christian nation and remains one to this day. Our problem is that we are too concerned about the feelings of the minority people who could care less about our own feelings. Political correctness has weakened this country so that the minority rules.

I can't imagine how the Glenside Kid would have grown up without the guidance of the good people at Carmel. It was, like the rest of my hometown, a great and positive place to grow up.

Somewhere along the way both the people who make decisions in the government and those who steer the ship of religion in the church seem to have lost their way. I pray that they find it again, though I'm not sure what it will take. Are we better off being less church focused? Of course not. How sad.

Chapter XLVI - The things we did for a buck

My first real job was working for the newspaper. I served the *Philadelphia Evening and Sunday Bulletin* as a newspaper carrier. And, hey, it wasn't as glamorous as it sounds.

The headquarters (they called it "the branch") was located in a white garage on Keswick Avenue, above Mt. Carmel. So, before I even got my papers to deliver I had a pretty good trek from home on my bicycle. Mix in rainy days (when you had to wrap the papers in plastic), cold days, brutally hot days, and it was a tough way for a kid to make a buck.

My friend and Oak Road neighbor David Gillum was a few years older than me and had been a paper boy for quite some time when he asked me if I'd like to substitute for him on his route. David, a straight arrow if there ever was one, was going to attend the Boy Scout Jamboree in Irvine, California. It was 1953, I was 12.

To get ready to fill in for two weeks, that was the deal, I did his route with him a few times. It seemed easy enough and so I said I'd do it. He paid me, too – plus I got to keep the tips, such as they were.

From being David's substitute it was a short jump to having my own route and it didn't take me long to decide that I did not like it very much. Factor in the aforementioned bad weather (though my Mom would drive me, if she could, on the rainy days and, usually, on Sunday) and the chronic non payers and you had a bad experience going.

I would go to collect from my customers every other Friday. The deal was, the paper boy actually paid the *Bulletin* for the papers and then it was up to them to collect the money and keep the commission plus whatever tips their benevolent clients could spare. If the paper was a dime, it cost me six cents (more on Sunday), you get the idea. Each customer owed me around a dollar-a-week if they got all seven papers, so when I collected on alternate weeks I was

The Glenside Kid

looking to collect two bucks, tops, when I knocked on their doors. In the meantime, I was on the hook for lots of money if they didn't pay.

"Nearly Everybody reads the Bulletin"

You'd be amazed, or maybe you wouldn't, at the number of people who would hide from me when I came to collect. I'd know they were in there, sometimes I could hear the radio, see the TV flickering, but they wouldn't answer the door. A few times I had to bring my enforcer, and Mom would bang on their doors until they answered.

I endured this for almost two years when I decided that the aggravation wasn't worth the few bucks I made. When I quit they offered to make me an 'assistant branch manager" but I was too smart for that, because what it really meant was that in addition to your own route if some other kid didn't show you got to do his or her route too – and then you had to collect from them to boot. It was the first, but not the last, executive position I would decline in my career.

The flower business calls on me

My friend, Bobby Wambold, worked for Muller's Flowers which was a large garden center operation right up Limekiln Pike, just past Beaver College and adjacent to the Catholic cemetery. Lots of dead – and remembered Catholics – made for big money on holidays and at funerals. He told me that there was a job opening there and that he would recommend me. I was 15, but I'd be 16 in the fall and driving and figured this job would allow me to build up some cash for my car.

I rode my bike to Muller's one Saturday in April and applied for the job, just in time for Easter. George M. Muller, a strict, ultra serious, German was the owner. He hired me on the spot when I assured him I'd be driving by the fall. He offered me 75-cents-an-hour – the minimum wage at the time. Wow, but that was more than the fifty cents-an-hour I was getting as an itinerant neighborhood babysitter, so I took it.

Bobby made sure that I got all the crummy jobs that he used to do. I was lugging top soil, carting flower pots, dragging flats of flowers and, once in a while, I actually got to wait on a customer. Of course if the customer bought something heavy I'd get to lug it to their car for them.

The part I liked the best was when I'd go out on the delivery truck with Angelo, an Italian guy – he must have been 80 and I have no idea what his last name was, they call called him "Angie". I was Angie's legs. He'd drive to wherever the flowers were destined and then I would carry them from the truck to wherever they were going. In the fall, when Angelo vanished from Muller's (we always suspected that George killed him – they used to yell at each other, one in Italian, the other in German, and we'd only guess what they were saying Bobby always opined that George buried him in a mulch pile someplace), I got to drive the delivery van as a one-man show. I had a license for about a month and here I was driving flowers all over the place. Was I nuts? Was Mr. Muller? Probably both of us were.

The Glenside Kid

Anyone who knows me well knows that my sense of direction isn't the keenest on the planet and so a delivery that should take a half hour in and out often ran to two or three hours as I cruised the city hunting for landmarks. The idea of a GPS then wasn't even in the sci fi comics. I'd come back and Mr. Muller would shout, "Where the hell have you been? I got more orders for you to deliver."

One day I drove down through Mt. Airy, then on to the Lincoln Drive toward East Falls, in the flower truck. I didn't know that trucks were verboten on that highway and the next thing you know a Philly cop and I are having a discussion on the side of the road – his cruisers red lights flashing, for me, an annoying staccato of despair.

The cop saw how young I was, how scared I was, and even how lost I was and gave me both a warning – and directions to my destination. Soon after that I relinquished the driving job. I was probably costing Muller a fortune in gas for all my lost trips.

But before I called it a career at Muller's I had one of those lifetime highlight-reel moments.

As grumpy and frightening as George was, the rest of his family was nice and he even had a cute daughter named Elsa. Well here I was wheeling a huge wheel barrow load of clay flower pots from the deep recesses of the Muller complex when I spied Elsa. I smiled, she waved, I waved back. Whoops!

When I waved I removed one of the two hands holding the wheel barrow upright and before I realized it the whole stupid load of clay flower pots was tumbling on to the macadam driveway – shattering as they hit. I probably destroyed half the load. Shortly after that my days at Muller's ended.

I'm going to sell Christmas trees

That winter I went in to the Christmas tree business. Well actually I became an employee of someone who was already in the business. And guess who got me the job? Yep, Bobby Wambold. I should have known better. How did he find these jobs?

Al Worthington, a short, muscular and rough looking guy, annually ran a Christmas tree business on the grounds of the Glenside Railroad station. He'd set up right after Thanksgiving and go, full tilt, until Christmas eve. You know the term 24/7? Well Al lived it for that month. His green wood and tar paper shack at the top of the hill – with the white sign proclaiming "Christmas Trees, Wholesale & Retail" - seemed to be open at all hours of the day and night and boy did he sell loads of Christmas trees.

The going rate was, again, 75-cents-an-hour, but the odds of making additional tip money, Bobby suggested, were much better than at Muller's. So I became a Christmas tree salesman or whatever Al wanted me to do when I showed up for work. There was usually more "whatever" than sales it seemed. As usual I was the youngest guy in the crew.

My work day usually started around 4 PM on weekdays – right after school - and lasted until about 10 PM. Mom would pack a dinner for me and I'd steal moments between chores to eat it. Weekends I worked 12-to-14 hours. I grew to hate Christmas trees and, to this day, when someone comments on how nice an evergreen smells I cannot smell them.

One of the parts of the job I hated the most was when Al would send me to unload a box car load of trees parked on a siding just up Glenside Avenue – cut the bundles and then bring them to the sales areas.

Outside the shed Al had a large steel drum in which he burned pieces of trees endlessly – and generated some considerable

The Glenside Kid

heat for us. Inside the shed he had an electric heater which, my bet was, he was plugging in to the Reading railroad's electrical outlet.

At the box cars it was cold – and it was dark. And the trees were packed in snow. It was Canadian snow, that's where he got his trees – shipped from Canada. Canadian snow seems colder. It was where I had my first drink of liquor. All the grownups working for Al had flasks and they'd share the contents with Bobby and me and a couple of other kids who worked there, Rye whiskey does an amazing job of warming you up.

When we'd find a scrawny tree Al would have us cut it up for "greens". In other words if he couldn't sell you that tree he'd sell you pieces of it so you could make a wreath out of it.

It was approaching Christmas when Al called us all together to tell us that he was having a really good year and, because of that, we could free-lance some of the harder-to-move trees. In other words, if we could sell certain ones that were still hanging around, we could name our own price and keep all the money. If the tree was small, or fat, or whatever and had sat there forever with a $10 price tag on it we were now permitted to sell it for five bucks or whatever we could get – and the money was ours.

There was one tree; it had to be 25-feet tall. It was shaped perfectly and Al had it tied and suspended in the middle of things. It showed nicely, but there's not much of a market of 25-foot-tall trees. And I was on duty one afternoon when an elderly, well-dressed, African American man approached me.

"I am looking for a nice tree for our church sanctuary," he said. "Do you have anything that would not be lost in the church?" And boy did I have such a tree. I told the man, who turned out to be a minister, to follow me and took him to the huge tree. His eyes lit up, "That's perfect," he said, "How much?"

Without batting an eye I said, "The boss was asking forty bucks for it (which, in fact, he was – and wasn't getting it) but since it's for a church I'm sure you could have it for $25."

"You've got a deal," he said and peeled off five fives and handed them to me. They went right in my pocket.

I tied up the tree and we carried it to his car which was a big black-and-silver Lincoln. The tree hung over the front and the back as he drove away. He blessed me and wished me a Merry Christmas which, of course, his twenty five bucks would help come true.

I never told Al exactly how much I got, I just acknowledged that I got rid of that big tree and made myself a few bucks in the bargain. I did tell Bobby and a few others – and they were green with envy.

When my college days began I didn't want to waste time – and freezing my fanny – selling trees and so I became a government employee. I got a job as a Christmas mailman.

In those days the post office would hire college kids home on Christmas break to supplement the regular mailman. It was the 1950's and the postal service was doing twice-daily deliveries for Christmas and paying a nice buck – about four times-an-hour more than Al Worthington or George Muller.

I was still out in the elements but for the extra dough it didn't seem as cold or uncomfortable as those other jobs. I even got to go home for lunch; I was, after all, now a government employee.

My route was in the Twickenham section of Glenside – lots of hills and houses not exactly close to one another. The most memorable stop was a large house located about the middle of my route. The attraction here was a ferocious dog that would bark at my daily arrival. I'm sure he'd have eaten me if he got loose.

The Glenside Kid

Well among our instructions from the post master was that the mail had to go in to either a mailbox or a mail slot in the door. We were not, under any circumstances, to leave it loose on the front stoop or porch. So the routine I developed with Mr. Nasty Dog was that I'd feed him the mail one letter at a time. I'd stick it in the slot, he'd grab it – we'd have a small tug-of-war - and when he won he'd do whatever dogs do with mail. Then we'd do it again.

Hey, sometimes you have to make your own fun when you work

Chapter XLVII – Face Book, who needs it?

My life has been like a Jean Shepherd story - complete with the cast of characters that inspire you and leave you with memories you'll never forget.

One recent Saturday evening we invited my lifelong friend Chuck Danihel and his wife Jane over for dinner – we get together far too seldom now despite the fact that we've known each other for most of our lives. It's ironic and kind of sad, but of all the kids that I grew up with and shaped my childhood he is the only one that remained in the neighborhood.

First we had cocktails and some snacks. Brett and Colleen were there with the twins and Little Lily managed to spit up all over Jane's dress as she was feeding her. A nurse, Jane didn't flinch.

Cindy made Swedish meatballs and Chuck showed that he had lost none of his youthful appetite. It always makes my wife happy when dinner guests go back for seconds – and even thirds.

People say that "Face Book" and the rest of the so-called social media is a good way to stay in touch – but I prefer doing it in person.

One friend said that the best thing about the social media is that it allows you to connect with people you haven't seen in decades. My answer to that is that if I haven't seen them in decades I probably have no interest in connecting with them or seeing them now.

But I'm not of the technological persuasion so what do I know?

On the other hand an evening with Chuck and Jane is one well spent and we really need to do it more often.

Chapter XLVIII - Chuck, Charlie, Cholly & Charles

Charles Danihel was ten when he moved to Glenside – I was twelve. The Danihel family consisted of him and his two parents. They lived in a single home the back yard of which was catty corned from ours. We alternately knew him as Charlie, Charles, Chuck or Cholly. Take your pick.

They say that where you live, who you know, what you experience all shape the way you end up. I buy that. If my life was a canvas, the portion that makes up my childhood would have the names of several kids that were part of my inner circle of friends. One very important person was Charles.

That's Chuck on the left blowing some music on his trumpet. It's New Year's Eve 1955. That's John Ewing on the other horn. And the back belongs to Karen Cliff. We were having a party.

He came to our town in time to be a fifth grader at Glenside School just as I was launching my career at Thomas Williams Junior High. We spent one year together at TW and one year at Cheltenham High.

We were like brothers during our childhood years. We even strung a tin can and string communications system between our houses. You stretch the string tight and you can actually talk to one another. How did that work? I haven't a clue, but it did. It wasn't great, mind you, but we actually used it. If we really wanted to talk with one another there was this other device in our house, a telephone, that provided clearer dialogue. No one had come up with e-mail, cell phones and every other "e" device that now muddies our world. I'm glad of that.

He was a musician of sorts and liked to play the trumpet. He did so in school and he did so at church. On summer nights, before the dawn of air conditioning, the entire neighborhood would be exposed to his endless practicing on his horn. No one would forget Harry James in favor of Chuck.

Chuck's father, a loud, kind of gruff (and a little scary) man put a basketball rim and net on their garage and the two of us played there endlessly. If it snowed we'd shovel it off and play. There was a floodlight out there too, so I'll bet the ka-thunking of the basketball probably drove the neighbor's nuts. His mom, Florence, was a nice lady and reminded me a little bit, later on when *All in the Family* was popular, of Edith Bunker in all the best ways.

His father was a member of a the Odd Fellows Lodge, a benevolent group that did good things for the underprivileged. I always thought he was a good fit for the group. Chuck belonged to the youth wing of that called deMolay. Today he's an Odd Fellow just like his father – no pun intended.

He was also a good all around athlete. A fine football player and a softball player who could hit the ball a mile for our Carmel Presbyterian team. He was, like me, an usher there as well.

Once in a YMCA church league basketball game Chuck, who was in a personal-problem-inspired bad mood, got called for a couple of fouls that he likely didn't really commit and when the ref – whom we agreed was blind-as-a-bat - put Chuck out of the game on a questionable fifth foul and he erupted.

The Glenside Kid

Chuck was bigger than the ref, bigger than all of us really, and he decided to vent his mounting frustration on the guy in the striped shirt. The ref, showing an incredible understanding of the situation, ran for his life. In fact he ran right out of the Abington YMCA and down Old York Road with Chuck chasing him and the rest of us chasing Chuck. Lucky for the ref we caught up to Chuck before he caught up to him. He's the only person I ever knew who was "banned for life" from a YMCA.

When we were in our late teens we actually started the Glenside Gorillas midget football club for which I got extra credit from the college since I was majoring in elementary education. We first played as an independent (the kids couldn't weigh more that 110 pounds and had to be no older than 13). The second season found us in the Keystone State League and we even had a "bowl game" in Albany NY where we scored first but then not often enough – and lost. Highlight of that trip was a parade through the center of Albany – Chuck and I each rode in the back of a convertible.

From that little venture (begun in 1958) has sprung the Glenside Youth Activities Organization and, ironically, they no longer have a football team.

He was a year older than my sister and always at my house. I think she'd have liked it if he showed a little interest in her other than as his friend's sister. But he never did.

But what do I remember most about Chuck?

Easy.

Every morning, regular as clockwork, he had the same breakfast. So what? You are probably thinking. Well, his daily breakfast consisted of a Coca Cola and, for extra nutrition, a donut. He was a big kid and, though younger, looked older. This came in handy when, as teenagers, we felt the need for a six-pack of beer and would dispatch Chuck in to the local deli on Mt. Carmel Avenue to get one. No one ever carded him.

A third member of our group was Bill Robinson. Bill was a Carmel guy and two years older than me – which meant he also had his own car, a vintage blue Chrysler. So Bill mostly drove.

We loved to bowl and haunted the Lynn Lanes bowling alleys on Cheltenham Avenue in Lynnewood Gardens. At the Pennsauken Bowling lanes across the Tacony Palmyra Bridge in New Jersey you could bowl all night – starting at midnight for a couple of bucks and we did that several times.

As teenagers we once went in to downtown Philly to be in the audience of a late night Channel 17 TV show, televised from a studio in the Suburban Station Building. Called "The Eddie Newman Show" – the host was a Philadelphia used car dealer who bought the air time – and we were among a dozen or so people in the bleachers. The "Diamonds", a popular signing group were his guests that night. As an extra bonus each audience member was given a salami. We left the show at mid-night and walked down Pennsylvania Boulevard tossing our salamis in to the air. I didn't even like salami.

He also had an uncle, Claude, who owned a used car business. The sign over his desk read "You can fool some of the people some of the time, and that's good enough for us". His uncle kept him in used cars and some of them occasionally even worked. When I was in college I bought a 1951 Pontiac from Uncle Claude. It was a tank disguised as a car. It was green, sort of metallic in color, and had the Indian head on the hood ornament. The radio didn't work so I went to a junk yard and bought one that did.

Claude was the kind of uncle kids liked to have. When he wasn't selling used cars he was running a restaurant. He lived in Melrose Park, a prosperous section of Cheltenham Township. One time, as I recall, he came up with the largest mechanical Santa Claus I ever saw. It looked lifelike and he had it in the picture window of

The Glenside Kid

his house. Where he got it I don't recall, but we all talked about it a lot.

With all his adventurous tendencies, Chuck became an accountant.

Chapter XLIX – Time marches on

After dinner the four of us retired to the living room. We were content and full from a delicious dinner – topped off by a Boston Crème Pie and coffee.

Chuck had brought along the 50th reunion yearbook from his class get-together in the spring. We enjoyed looking at it remembering all the "kids" we both grew up with. Even my old girl friend Ginny was in there.

Like our class (our 50th was two years ago) there were a lot of deceased classmates – making you aware of your own mortality - whom we could only remember from their high school yearbook pictures. When you are living those days they seem like they will last forever – and then you look around and wonder where it all went.

Life is, after all, a celebration. We start as babies, become little kids, grow in to adults – all the while shaping ourselves and our futures.

The twins are at the threshold of something wonderful. It's the starting point and, for them, the sky is the limit. Hopefully we'll get to spend a lot of time with them and share the kinds of memories that our elders crafted for us.

Getting older is not exactly for the timid. On the other hand it sure beats the alternative.

The Glenside Kid

Chapter L - The past is prologue

My three high school years flew by pretty quickly – and the decade of the 1950's was gone before I realized it. I was CHS Class of 1958. I had a lot of friends at Cheltenham High; somehow I even managed to pass everything, played some sports, did the student council bit and generally enjoyed my life.

One day I'm a sophomore, overwhelmed by the huge college-like campus in Elkins Park that was Cheltenham High School and the next I'm taking Ginny to the Meadowlands Country Club in Pop's '58 Caddy for our senior prom. The last significant event in my high school career – except, of course, for commencement.

At CHS I played football for two seasons – running cross country as a senior so that I might actually live to go to college. I became a harrier out of necessity, having been knocked silly in the last football game of my junior year. Richard Delaney was the coach and he coerced me in to running for him when he found out I wasn't playing football any more. I hated cross country. Hated it!

I loved football even if I was really too small to be good. The main thing, a moment really, I'll always remember about playing high school football and that was the moment before each home game when we all ran down the hill from the locker room, crossed High School Road, and entered the football field. The band was playing, the fans were cheering and we were the stars of the moment. Heady stuff, indeed.

We were way ahead of the curve at CHS. Our quarterback in my sophomore year was black. His name was Freddy Robinson and he was good, too. We also had a soccer player as kicker, Bill Friebel – and one day he had a home soccer game going on one field and our football game on the other. He kicked off in his soccer uniform. The biggest kids at CHS, it seemed, were always in the marching band.

I tried a little culture at high school too. I took Miss June Taylor's "Music Appreciation" class in my senior year. I had some electives to fill and figured this to be a snap "A" – and it was. I know Miss Taylor tried to fill our heads with new music ideas, but most of us were there for only for the fun of it – we were rock 'n roll music aficionados. She loved the classics, and once played some music by an opera singer named Lucia Albanese (pronounced Al-ban-ay-zee). When I suggested we form a fan club Miss Taylor thought there was hope for me yet. For the next class I had cooked up signs and posted them around the room saying "We all go crazy for Lucia Albanese". She was not amused. I got the A anyway.

I passed biology thanks to Barbara Thomas and Eleanor Sizemore. In fact all three of us got A's because our biology teacher was too lazy to grade test papers and, instead, told us to swap papers and grade each others. Barbara, Eleanor and I switched alright – and at the end of the switch we had our own papers back. Didn't know any answer? Leave it blank. The teacher will give it when we're grading papers and we can fill it in. After the grading was done by us, he collected the papers duly marked the grades in his roll book. I'm told that students had been doing that for years in his class.

Ralph Luef taught me to type – it was another elective. We called him "Roving the keys Ralph". He seemed as though he was 70, probably wasn't and he was a sweet man. Another A, thank you. He taught me to type the correct way, but I could always go faster with the Biblical system – "Seek and ye shall find".

And so went high school.

I applied to and got accepted by several colleges but I knew that where I'd go was to a place that my family could afford and it was also the first college that accepted me, Millersville State Teachers College.

College was always my mother's goal for me, but to be honest I wanted to be like my Pop's cousin Commander Rusty Ruestle USN. I idolized Rusty and he spent a lot of time with me

The Glenside Kid

whenever he was home visiting his parents – Pop's sister (Elsie) and her husband (Jim).

Rusty had been a combat diver in World War II and now was a diving instructor for the Navy and got lots of sweet assignments all over the globe. He always had a nice home, drove the best cars, dressed like a millionaire. He told me that if I joined the Navy they'd likely send me to officer's training school and I'd have a good career.

I liked the idea and, one day, confided in Pop that I was considering the Navy rather than college. He got a stern look on his face and said "Let's talk" and took me in to my room and closed the door. I knew I was in for a lecture.

"Personally I'd be fine with you joining the Navy," he said, "But your mother has her heart set on your going to college and so I'm telling you, don't disappoint her and join the service." (My timing was such, as it turned out, that I'd have probably ended up in Viet Nam had I joined the Navy.)

And so I graduated from Cheltenham High, had a nice summer mostly in Ocean City with my friends, and prepped for college. The Navy was off the table. Mom never knew, at least she never commented. I did join the Air National Guard while in College and the Viet Cong never occupied Lackland AFB base in Texas where I trained. I guess I did my job. I got mustered out early. I was not mechanically inclined and they wanted more mechanics, not guys who could write. I still belong to the American Legion.

The Glenside Kid's growing up journey really ends with a trip to Lancaster County PA. It's September, 1958, and I'm on my way to college – Millersville to be specific. I decided to major in elementary education because (a.) I liked little kids and (b.) I had been told that older kids could be a real pain and (c.) I was told, by my Pop, that I needed to do something that entailed using my brain because I was a klutz when it came to anything mechanical or working with my hands.

The Glenside Kid

I went to Millersville because, among other things, my family could afford it. My Mom had diligently saved all the Social Security checks that she had received for my care since 1949 (when my father died) and now they had grown in to a pretty substantial nest egg. I had no idea she had done that until my step-father told me during our Navy vs. college lecture.

Cheltenham High School had well prepared me for college. It was an elite high school and 95 per cent of my class mates went on to college (the rest actually joined the service, one went to jail for murder).

Our neighbor, Dr. Harting, told me there was a trick to taking college entrance exams – there were no college boards yet, you took a separate entrance test for every college. I learned the tricks from him and aced entrance exams for Millersville, William & Mary, Syracuse, Ohio State and even Penn. I really couldn't afford any of them but Millersville and so the testing was more a lark than a quest.

Millersville meant leaving my girlfriend Ginny and my closest pal Chuck. She was a junior at Cheltenham, so was he. I'd miss Chuck, but I'd really miss Ginny. I swore to her that I'd get home most weekends and pretty nearly did. You could stand out in front of Old Main on Friday afternoon with your thumb out and get a ride to the vicinity of Glenside. It never failed. On Sunday nights I'd always ride back with someone from the area. Lots of us bailed out on weekends, it seemed.

College loomed as an adventure and I was ready for it. Early that summer I got a letter from the dean of men telling me that my new roommate was going to be a kid named Tom Franks. I didn't know it at the time, but I must have lost that lottery big time. Colleges always try to match you up with someone compatible. This match wasn't even close. Tom was an orphan. He was on a scholarship from the Milton Hershey School and he, charitably,

The Glenside Kid

marched to his own drummer. We had one thing, only, in common. We were both guys.

Millersville State Teacher's College – Old Main is in the foreground

My first dorm room was 492 in Old Main – a creaky old building that was the original structure on campus. The floors moaned, the lights flickered and our beds were military surplus bunks still painted gray from when they slept sailors at some World War II Naval base. Oh yes, they were uncomfortable as could be. You could make them singles or leave them as bunks. We opted for singles on opposite sides of the room. We each had a bureau and a desk. Luxurious it was not.

The bathroom was down at the end of the linoleum covered hall. The hallway itself was always cold. The showers were gang showers and there was one stinking pay phone on the whole floor. Sometimes it rang-and-rang nobody bothered answering it. Odds were that the call wasn't for you anyway. They would, occasionally spring a fire alarm on us in the middle of the night. I guess they were being cautious, the old building was a tinder box. You got laundry service. The deal was you clipped your clothes – underwear, whatever, together with a big safety pin that had your name on it and dumped it down the laundry shoot – every once-in-a-while we also dumped a kid down the chute. A few days later you could go pick it up, the laundry not the kid. What happened was, I think, was that they boiled all the clothes because by the end of the year my skivvies were falling apart. Mostly I took my good stuff home for Mom to wash.

When you arrived on campus they gave you a "dink" which was a black cap with a gold button on it and a badge with your name on it. You were to wear these all over campus and when an upper classman said, "Button's Frosh" you were expected to lift the cap from your head and reply "We love the upper classmen". It was a lie, of course, we didn't love them.

About a week in to that nonsense several of us realized that the caps equaled abuse and if you didn't wear one they left you alone. We lost ours, never to be worn again.

Incoming freshmen got their schedules handed to them upon arrival which virtually assured a lot of crappy class times. I had early classes – big gaps in the middle of the day with nothing to do, so I played a lot of ping pong – and then late classes. I usually cut the late class on Fridays to catch a ride home, mostly to see Ginny. The Professor for that Friday class didn't seem to care since I was there the other two days of the week.

The dining hall was on the far side of the campus – and I hardly ever made it there for breakfast subsisting, instead, on a ration of cheese crackers and orange-flavored Tang that mom gave me to bring back with me on each of my visits home. She also supplied "Fizzies" which, when dropped in a glass of water, became some kind of soda drink – kind of like Alka Seltzer with a flavor.

One of the ongoing staples for dinner at the dining hall was "mystery burgers". We knew they were some kind of meat – and most of us actually developed a tolerance, if not a taste, for them. We never were quite sure what the meat really was, but beef got very few votes in our survey. Being on the baseball team got me a

The Glenside Kid

pass to the "training table" in the second semester which translated in to you could eat as much as you wanted and, occasionally, it was better than – and certainly more of - what the mere peons were eating.

There was a greasy spoon near our dorm called "The Sugar Bowl". It still exists to this day – and it is still a greasy spoon. I ate many a meal there, certainly bought lots of snacks from them. I could see "The Bowl" from my dorm window and, if at dinner time, there was a line down George Street you knew, darn well, that whatever the dining hall was serving no one was eating it. The longest lines occurred when the dining hall served liver. I didn't like liver when my Mom made it, I sure wasn't going for it at Millersville.

About 1,200 students made up the entire population of the college and the President, Dr. Donald L. Biemesderfer, knew everyone by name by the start of the second semester. That really freaked me out when I was walking across campus one day in February and he addressed me by name 'Good morning, Mr. Taylor" he said. Good lord, he knows me!

The Glenside kid makes the college ball club

Hal Weirich was assistant dean of men, in charge of our dorm, and he was also baseball coach. Hal was a cool guy, I liked him, he liked me. Once, when my pal Harry "The Hammer" Finlayson and I got caught visiting a couple of coeds in the girl's side of Old Main we got off with a "never do that again" instead of the suspension that the student hand book called for. It didn't hurt that Harry and I were on the baseball team – and that Hal understood what raging hormones were like in college men. Both of us busted our tails to make the team, practice began outdoors in February, and the coach appreciated the effort – I suppose.

Professors are quirky people just like high school teachers and I didn't take me long to figure that out. Our Ed Psych professor, Dr. Jacob Heckler, had a text book written by Smith & Smith and the man, for the life of him couldn't remember the second "Smith". He'd say "Now let's turn to page so and so in our book by Smith and, err, ah, umm…oh yes, Smith". He wasn't kidding, he was serious.

Our little old Pennsylvania Dutch speech teacher, Miss Obermeyer, once floored us all by saying that she was retiring next year. She added, "I may die an old maid, but I won't die a virgin". Wowser!

Football coach George Katchmer hounded me to play football for the Marauders because he knew I played in high school. I told him that I was 140 pounds soaking wet and really would like to live to graduate. He always laid guilt on me, "You are letting your school down" and, that being the case, so I did.

Law enforcement in the actual town of Millersville was the responsibility of one man – they called him "Charlie the cop". We'd meet Charlie at the end of George Street furthest from the campus where an old taproom called "The Hotel" was located. We were all under-aged, but Charlie didn't care as long as we behaved. What trouble could you possibly get in to in Millersville? I drank so much beer at the Hotel that I dislike it now and have for most of my adult life.

The Glenside Kid

The rules also said that you couldn't have a car on campus if you were a freshman – and so for the first semester most of us didn't have one. I commuted home a lot that first year. Less after Ginny's mother succeeded in breaking us up. But I maintained a life in Glenside that was parallel to the one I was living in Lancaster County.

But in the spring, when I was playing baseball, it was handy to have a car there and so I parked the one I bought from Uncle Claude a couple of blocks from the campus and no one ever figured that out – or if they did, they didn't care.

A member of my circle of college friends, Claude Rothermel Ulmer, was a fun kid and a car nut and said he'd be bringing his hot rod back from Minersville, where he lived, after the Christmas holidays. It was a super-charged Ford something. Big engine, lots of speed. Claude hit – and sheared off – a bunch of trees doing about 100 MPH while he was home and neither he or the car ever made it back for the second semester. He was buried over the holidays. We all went to the funeral. Death claimed yet another member of the cast.

Getting back to Tom Franks. Being a Lancaster County boy he explained how you could turn apple cider in to something more lethal if you let it ferment outside in the sun. He did just that and then drank the concoction that resulted - and he almost died. I came back from class one day and he was just laying there in bed moaning. I quick ran and got Coach Weirich.

Tom spent a few days in the infirmary with some kind of alcohol poisoning, the result of his drinking binge. An orphan and lifelong dorm student, and resourceful in so many ways, he also had a hot plate in the room – against college rules – and was always cooking something. Each day he'd dump the grease from the hot plate in to the rain spout outside our window. When the gutters clogged and they traced the grease back to room 492 Tom was in big trouble. By the second semester Tom was my ex-roomie and Harry the Hammer and I shared a much better room on the first floor of the dorm. Tom got a single, he was happy. So was I.

Driver's Ed was a big deal then and Coach Hal taught it. We all took the course as one of our electives so we could be certified to teach that extra course when we graduated. I was an elementary ed major, who was I going to teach to drive at my school? But I took it anyway. It made Hal happy.

Elementary Ed majors taught, first, in something called "The Lab School". The kids there, local town children, were subjected to endless and an ever changing cast of MSTC students trying their hands at teaching. I wonder if any of them ever really learned anything.

You grow up a lot in college. You make friends, you lose friends. Romances die. Time does that, different situations reinforce your need for independence. By the end of that first year, the Glenside Kid was, at the very least, the Glenside young man. When I headed back to Glenside at the end of my freshman year I was a different person and a new set of life stories were lurking. New experiences, new challenges. But the Kid was on his way to being a grown-up. Life would never be the same again.

Going away to college does that.

The Glenside Kid

Book Two.....

The Glenside Kid Rides Again!

The Glenside Kid

Chapter One – Rocking my world

Some may feel that this second book doesn't even belong here. it really isn't part of my growing up story, but, on the other hand, maybe it really is. It certainly is about living and it's something that I felt the need to share with my readers. I've included this section in my book because, to quote my wife, "You can't write about just the fun things, you need to deal with the bigger picture" and, you know I believe she is right.

Over eleven years ago my longtime friend and physician Dr. Michael Lyons rocked my world when he told me he had discovered, what he believed to be, cancer in my body.

It had came up in a routine examination and he immediately started the ball rolling for me to learn exactly what I was up against.

I don't remember much that was said after I heard the word "cancer" but I know I told the doctor that I needed to deal with this, "I really don't have time to fool around, I am too busy with life," I said.

It was February of 2000 I learned that I wasn't bullet proof after all. We all think we're immortal, you know. What follows is the story of how I dealt with cancer – the same disease that took my father's life when he was much too young.

After I did all my due diligence about the disease I told Dr. Lyons that not only was I going to follow a different path of treatment than he had advised, but I was also going to chronicle the experience for publication.

He essentially told me I was "nuts". He said, "That's a very private thing, don't you think it would be better if you didn't go public with it?"

The Glenside Kid

I'm a public kind of guy and a writer. I told him that if I get the story in front of people maybe it will help them deal with it. The Montgomery newspapers ran it as an eight-parter (running November-December, 2001). Abington Hospital put it on it's website and it has helped a lot of people I've been told. Later Dr. Lyons has even told me, basically, I was right to do it.

As a result of my experiences I believe that I have helped others. I have counseled people one-on-one, I have spoken to service clubs and hospital seminars.

What follows is my story about cancer and how it didn't ready didn't stand a chance against "The Glenside Kid".

Chapter Two - The "Kid" does battle with Cancer

"You have a serious health issue that we need to discuss", said Dr. Michael Lyons as I walked in to his Glenside office on February 28, 2000 for, what I thought was going to be the results of my annual routine physical.

The office had always been a place of comfort to me. The stately old house on Easton Road, the paneled walls, the familiarity of a place where I had been going for my health care since I was a toddler.

Those few words stunned me, eventually rearranged my life and sent me on a seven-month physical and emotional journey that I had never even considered before.

Most people take good health for granted. You live each day as if you are immortal. In my life I have been in the hospital overnight just twice. Once when I was five to have my tonsils removed, once 20 years ago for a double hernia. I don't like hospitals. I don't even like to visit them when somebody else is sick.

In preparation for my regular annual physical Dr. Lyons had sent me to have a series of blood tests at Abington Hospital the week before.

My relationship with Dr. Lyons goes back many years. My relationship with his office goes back further. As a small child Dr. Karl Mayer treated me from that office at 255 N. Easton Rd. in Glenside. Later on, from that office, Dr. Mayer's nephew Donald treated my family and me. And then, Dr. Lyons succeeded Dr. Don in the practice and became both our family physician and friend.

I always look forward to my checkups with him. They are usually lighthearted and carefree but this day he met me in the hallway and told me that he wanted to discuss "a serious health issue" with me. Oh boy.

The Glenside Kid

I really never have had a serious health issue before so I wasn't very good at anticipating what was coming next. He cut right to the chase. In my series of tests was a PSA (prostate-specific antigen) test for prostate cancer. The prostate is walnut-sized gland that makes a fluid that is part of semen. The normal reading is 4.0, mine was 4.9. (The last time it was taken, two years ago, it was 2.9.) He told me that *I might* have prostate cancer or it *might* simply be an enlarged prostate. He told me that regardless of what I was doing the next day I had to stop doing it and plan on seeing Dr. John Mandler at Suburban Urological at 2:15 PM.

I was not emotionally prepared to learn that I might have prostate cancer. No one ever wants to hear that dreaded word in a sentence that has to do with him or her. It is the great unknown. But once I was faced with it I hit it head on. In this series I will detail how someone, like me, dealt with the news, researched my options and successfully battled the fears and uncertainty sparked by the most dreaded six-letter word in our vocabulary.

Some of my closest friends tried to discourage me from writing this. They said I'd be exposing myself to the public. That people would "know my business". But I finally decided to write this because it might help someone else deal with it. And despite all of the research I did, I was never able to find a single first-hand account of how someone like me handled this. My decision has been borne out over the years as this has been published at the Abington Hospital website, run as an eight-part series in the local newspaper and led me to address groups and counsel individuals who, at best, are scared of the unknown – at worst terrified of it.

My wife Cindy has been a rock of support. She had lost her Mother to lung cancer a few years before and I was afraid of how she'd react when I told her of my problem, but she handled it in such a supportive way and was all for me putting my thoughts down on paper. My three sons - who now have to face the fact that, besides my baseball card collection, they might inherit this - have been very strong and caring supporters. My daughter probably took it the hardest, but she's the baby of the family and didn't want her Daddy to be sick.

Prostate Cancer is not selective. It strikes males, mostly over 50, and anyone it pleases. No one is even sure what causes it. Onetime New York Yankee manager Joe Torre has had it and has an informative website. On that site and he reflects on how he and his wife dealt with the news and faced adversity together. But Joe is a celebrity and his issues were a little different than mine - at least that's what I got out of his writings. Charlton Heston had it (Moses, imagine that) and former Felipe Alou another former baseball star and manager has dealt with it too. And, as the months unfolded, I found out that a staggering number of average guys, like me, are dealing with it or will be facing it shortly.

On the day Dr. Lyons told me of my potential problem he also told me lots of other things I needed to know. I didn't remember any of them. Not after hearing the word "Cancer". That's the kind of a word that shuts down your brain. My mind went in to over-drive. My Father had died of "Cancer" in 1949 at age 42. That was what I was thinking. Oh brother, I'm doomed and I'm not ready to be doomed. I have too many things to do.

Prostate cancer is found most often in men over 50. More than 80 per cent of those with prostate cancer are over age 65 (I was the same age as Joe Torre was when he discovered it - 60). They will diagnose 180,000 new cases of prostate cancer each year and the disease will claim 30,000 annually. It is the second leading cause of cancer death for men in this country, which is why early detection is so important.

Right after dropping that news on me Dr. Lyons took my blood pressure. It was through the roof. He mentioned that it was "a little high". I said it was a wonder his equipment counted that high. I don't deal well - blood pressure wise - with stress. My dentist, for example, refuses to take my blood pressure anymore.

The Glenside Kid

Chapter Three – Don't worry, it'll just feel like a pin prick

The very next day I visited with Dr. John I. "Jack" Mandler who is one of the top urologists in the country. Dr. Mandler is a surgeon and Dr. Lyons had told me that surgery was the best bet if it was, indeed, prostate cancer. I dreaded the "s" (surgery) word almost as much as the "c" word (cancer).

Twenty-plus years ago Dr. Mandler removed my wife's kidney stone, so we had a bit of family history with him. Dr. Mandler is noted for being gruff and to the point. He came by the reputation honestly. We chatted at some length. He told me about prostate cancer and how if mine was cancerous we had found it very, very early (just .9 over normal). He said the best way to find out was by taking a biopsy and he slated that for the following week.

Later that day Dr. Lyons called me on the phone and told me all the things that "he knew I hadn't heard" when I was in the office the day before. Among them he mentioned the possibility of treating this with radiation and told me that I had a lot of options and mentioned, again, "This will not be what kills you." He also repeated what he had told me in his office. It might be ten years before I even had any symptoms that men over 70 with other health problems seldom even get treated for it and, finally, more men die with it later in life than from it. He is a special doctor.

The biopsy was to be performed in Dr. Mandler's Abington Hospital office a week later. He told me that it would feel like a "pin prick" and when he did the first one I almost flew off the table. He asked if I was okay and I replied that I didn't know what kind of pins people had been pricking him with lately, but what he just did to me felt more like someone had clipped me with a pair of garden shears. He said the others wouldn't be as bad and he was right. (Of course, by comparison, once someone hits you over the head the first time the blows that follow are never quite as bad.) He said that it would hurt for awhile and to anticipate some bleeding in my urine. And boy did I get it. Then it cleared up and I was good to go. Then on Monday it (the bleeding) came back, strong as ever, and I was a

The Glenside Kid

wreck (there went the old blood pressure again) until Dr. Lyons prescribed some antibiotics to clear it up. (Dr. Mandler passed away a few years ago – from cancer.)

Another week passed and I went to Dr. Mandler's office and was hopeful he was going to tell me that I simply had an enlarged prostate - which is common as men get older. But, typical of his reputation, the first words out of his mouth were "it's malignant". Oh good, I thought. He then told me that it was tiny, located in the apex of my prostate (wherever that was) and that surgery would be the way to go. He then recited a number of evil sounding things that could befall me as a result of that surgery. Such pleasantries as incontinence, erectile dysfunction, problems with bowel function were at the top of the list. He asked me when I wanted to schedule the surgery. I told him I'd get back to him on that. Dr. Lyons' words "you have lots of options" were ringing in my ears.

As part of the whole package Dr. Mandler sent me to Holy Redeemer Hospital for a CAT scan to make sure that the cancer hadn't made inroads anyplace else. Up to the minute he mentioned that I had never even considered that potential added attraction. The CAT scan went well; I was in and out in a flash.

The good news from the CAT scan was that I was cancer free everywhere else but the old prostate and so my wife, Cindy, and I went to see Dr. Lyons to plot our strategy. He was still all for surgery. I said that I needed to know more about other treatments before I would push the surgery button. He said that was fine and sent me to Dr. Melvyn P. Richter, chief of Radiation Oncology at Abington Hospital's Rosenfeld Cancer Center. Dr. Richter was another heavyweight having once held the same position at Fox Chase Cancer Center. I'm sure that Dr. Lyons felt that once I heard about radiation that I'd still vote for surgery.

I liked Dr. Richter immediately. He was candid about the options I faced. He asked me about my family history and if there was any cancer in it. I told him that my father had died of cancer in 1949 but that I had no idea what kind of cancer it was. He concluded

The Glenside Kid

that it must have been colorectal and it may have been, but no family records exist and my sister Pat had no idea either. In those days you died of cancer, not lung cancer, colon cancer, pancreatic cancer, etc. I later mentioned that to Dr. Lyons who said that my father's cancer in 1949 really was not really a concern since treatment since then has come "light years". I hope so, that was 52 years ago.

In any event Dr. Richter noted that I was "clear thinking" (not everyone says that) and that everything else about me was fine (heart rate of 72, BP of 150/80) and so on.

Dr. Richter agreed that surgery would be an appropriate solution but noted that the location of the disease (right apex) that Dr. Mandler might need to modify his approach. He also noted that should I decide to go the radiation route, that he would recommend five weeks of conformal irradiation followed by brachytherapy (the implant of radioactive seeds directly in the prostate).

A few days later I met with Dr. Lyons again and told him that I still had doubts as to which way to go and he said, okay, go see his colleague Dr. Richard Greenberg, who is chief of urologic oncology at the Fox Chase Cancer Center. I said that would be a good plan and we set it. He was sending me to another surgeon, there was definitely a pattern emerging.

On April 11 I met with Dr. Greenberg who was cordial, informative and examined all the evidence. He checked the cat scans. He looked at the little pictures from the biopsy, he read the notes that Dr. Mandler and Dr. Richter had written to Dr. Lyons about me and then told me, in cold hard terms, what he thought about my problem. He said lots of things, told me of the surgical risks and then, mentioning that "apex" location (which, apparently is hard to access), and said to me, "I might tell you that surgery was the best way to go and then get you on the operating table, open you up, see the location of the problem, and decide that radiation was the better solution."

The Glenside Kid

That, for me, was the old ball game. Game, point, match. I told him "thanks" and said that as far as I was concerned no one was going to open me up surgically and then decide, "oh well, there's a better way".

Over the next four days I did hours and hours of research on the computer, called a friend at the American Cancer Society and spoke with three people that I knew who had had either the surgery, the implants or radiation. Only the one who had had the surgery could tell me any horror stories, five years after surgery he still was having problems with his urinary and sexual functions. I also spoke with two nurses who worked with my wife (she's in the healthcare field) and I did some serious soul-searching. Oh yes, I prayed pretty hard for guidance, too.

Chapter Four – We tell Dr. Lyons what the plan will be

When Cindy and I met with Dr. Lyons on April 16 I brought with me a seven-page document that I had worked on over the weekend. I drew up two columns, on one side were the pluses for surgery, on the other the minuses. I did the same for radiation. The conclusion was to do what Dr. Richter suggested, radiation first, seed implants next.

Among the minuses for surgery was the location of my lesion (that darned old apex), potential for long-term incontinence, impotence, bowel problems and overall quality of life in the future. There was the possibility, I was told at one point (and I don't even recall who told me anymore), that I would be unable to drive for up to 12 weeks after surgery, face a possible two-three week period of discomfort wearing a catheter and have a bag strapped to my leg. Nerve endings could be permanently damaged in surgery, a 30% chance that it will recur after surgery anyway and erectile dysfunction. In a nationwide survey, listed on the American Cancer Society webpage, I learned that only one in four patients chose surgery. The obvious (and lone, at least as I saw it) plus was that the prostate would be gone - surgically removed.

The minuses for radiation included the fact that localized cancer may recur and external beams can damage healthy tissue and impotence. The pluses were many. They destroy cancerous cells, shrinks tumors, often as effective as surgery. For the radioactive seeds the feeling in many circles is that this will become the accepted, most common form of prostate cancer treatment in this decade. I learned that seeds control growth in 85% of the men for ten years and produce fewer side effects than long-term beam radiation. Incontinence is rare.

Now I must tell you that I was uncomfortable telling Dr. Lyons that I was, basically, going against his initial recommendation. I trust him with my health and that of my family, but my research told me that I had made the right choice and he, himself, had told me earlier that I had a lot of options. It just

The Glenside Kid

happened the option that I chose wasn't the one he would have selected for me. Though I had chosen to disregard his opinion he now fully supported my decision and told me so.

Having gotten over that hump I was back in Dr. Richter's office a few days later and the wheels began rolling toward getting this problem of mine under control. He ordered an ultra-sound. It was at this meeting that I met Dr. Scott Herbert who was actually going to handle the radiation and seed implant treatment. We set a further "get acquainted" meeting for the following week.

This was called a Re-Con session. Dr. Herbert is a bright young radiation oncologist who guided me through the next few months with information and good humor. He sensed that I needed to take a light, yet informed approach and guided me in that direction. It turned out that one of his best friends was Jeff Kaplan, a man who was the CEO of the Fleer Corporation during part of the time that I was vice president of hobby sales, marketing and public relations for the sports card and confectionery giant based in Mt. Laurel, NJ. Small world, huh?

Throughout the month of May the tests and the examinations continued and I was getting to be such a familiar face at the Rosenfeld Cancer Center that the parking lot attendant asked me if I wanted to buy a discount package. I declined, said I'd see him later.

Toward the end of the month I had a session in which I actually went in to the radiation lab (LA 2) where they took x-rays and made a body cast of my posterior. (Imagine that, a plaster cast of your fanny). It was something that I would lie in 25 times over a five-week period of radiation. It felt kind of funny and warm. They stuck things in me, as usual, drew little x's on me and actually placed little tattoos that would direct the beam radiation. I was getting used to those ugly gray and yellow hospital gowns. They asked me when I would like to do my radiation. Then they gave me a little card that I had to run by a scanner each day when I arrived and then told me what time they had available. I love a democracy.

Right before the radiation treatments were to begin I paid another visit to Dr. Lyons. We talked about my experiences thus far and he gave me my regular checkup. Cholesterol was fine, BP fine; everything else was as good as it could be.

Chapter Five – I begin radiation treatments

For my first radiation treatment I came in having no idea what to expect. It was May 30. I didn't know how long it would be but I did learn that the valet parking people left at 5 PM so I got the bonus of being able to park anyplace I wanted and for free. They do radiation treatments to out patients at selected times during the day. My "selected time" came at days' end.

Anyone who experiences their treatments at Abington's Rosenfeld Cancer Center radiation facility is in for a satisfying experience. All of the technicians are caring, warm people. They realize, of course, that radiation treatments are no day in the park and they make it bearable. Mine were so brief in daily duration that it took me longer to get undressed and then dressed again than the treatments took. I met lots of interesting men over the next five weeks and we all shared our war stories. Some younger, some older. Some radiation veterans who were doing it again. But I never met anyone being treated for prostate cancer in my time slot. I thought that was strange. You see the same people every day and you strike up friendships. You are, after all, in the same boat.

Just as I was getting in to the routine of things and making sure that whatever business plans I had, I had to be back in Abington by 5 PM I found out that five days-a-week are not always a given. I was to be guest speaker at the Central Bucks High School baseball banquet at Pinecrest CC in Montgomeryville on June 5 and told them I might be a bit late. At 3 PM the hospital called and said their machinery was down, that I was going to have to skip that day. It was okay with me; I made the banquet on time. The daily treatments resumed the next day when the equipment was fixed.

I was surprised to learn that I needed an urologist to actually implant the radioactive seeds and, presto, I was on my way back to Dr. Mandler's office in mid June. He was going to get a piece of me after all. This time, however, the urologist I dealt with was Dr. Joseph K. Izes. He just wanted to meet me, say "hi" and probe my rectum. (Seems like that was a really popular place anymore.

The Glenside Kid

Everyone wanted to touch my lesion.) As luck would have it, there was also a resident in his office that day and, guess what, he wanted to probe it too. After he rooted around, for what seemed like ten minutes, I asked if he was looking for my wallet or what. The lesion was so small, so well tucked away, he couldn't find it.

On June 20 following the day's radiation I was told that Dr. Herbert wanted to see me and the next thing I knew he was simulating the implant procedure and sticking all kinds of scopes and probes in places where things are not comfortably stuck. Like a woman giving birth, I was on my back, and my legs were up in stirrups. Giddy-up. That day Dr. Herbert asked when would be a good time in August for me to have the seed implants. I told him anytime but the week of August 4-11 because we planned to be away on vacation. Of course a week later Dr. Izes' office called and told me that the procedure was set for August 8. Murphy's Law I guess.

Like anything repetitious the radiation treatments got old and so July 6 was a welcome day for me. It was my last one. Since I was leaving on vacation that night it was imperative that I get the final treatment in and as luck would have it the machine went down. I ended up getting my final treatment on another machine and this one scoped my whole lower body and kind of knocked me for a loop. It was the second time during my treatments that this had happened.

The most obvious side effect was that I tired more easily. I also had some discomfort with my bodily functions.

When we returned from vacation my wife baked a batch of cookies for the radiation staff and I happily delivered them to a very nice group of people.

Chapter Six – We enter the final phase

On July 20 I went to Dr. Izes' office for a cystoscopy. You don't want one of these things unless they are absolutely necessary. It is a long wiry scope that inserted in the end of your penis and Dr. Izes told me to take a deep breath as he inserted it. I was gasping at the time, so the deep breath just kind of evolved. If you grew up in my era the best way to describe the cystoscope is that it looks like Willie the Worm wearing a miner's lamp on his head. (Willie showed Farmer Alfalfa cartoons on early Philly TV and had an unseen helper named Newton the Mouse. Willie was a piece of pipe, the kind you vent your clothes drier with. It felt like Willie, Newton and Farmer Alfalfa himself had all gone inside of me.)

All my preliminary tests were coming out great and so on August 1 I had to check in at the Abington Hospital pre-admission center. The center is, literally, tucked behind the coffee wagon in the Shoreday lobby making it somewhat hard to find. But I found it. I needed to go through all the pre-admission testing to make sure that I wasn't falling apart elsewhere and could physically tolerate the exciting experience that they had planned for me the following week. My appointment was 8:45; they took me at 9:15, not that bad.

The staff was friendly and I sailed through my interview, EKG and chat with the anesthesiologist who told me that my seed implants would kind of simulate the childhood game of "Battleship". "There will be a grid on the screen and they will implant the seeds according to what they see on the grid," he said. My hope, of course, was that my battleship didn't get torpedoed. The chest x-ray part of the routine proved to be a bit of an ordeal. I ended up waiting about an hour in a waiting room that was a little short of seats and then for a few minutes more in a holding room that was fresh out of available lockers. Oh yes, they gave me directions as to where to go the following week - Fifth floor, Toll Building. The directions lead me to the basement. A janitor showed me how to find the right elevators and quipped "it happens all the time". Wonderful.

The Glenside Kid

The day before my implants I was a little confused. I got instructions from Dr. Mandler's office that said "don't eat anything for 24 hours before your procedure". I was only allowed clear liquid. On the other hand Dr. Richter's office said that I shouldn't eat anything after midnight the day of surgery (August 8). I compromised. I ate soup for lunch, had a light dinner. Both doctors said I did the right thing.

I woke up at 5 AM on the day of the procedure (August 8). We left for the hospital a 6 AM, got to the hospital at 6:10, realized that my medical card was home and went back and got it. At 6:20 we returned. After having gotten lost looking for the elevator, I finally made my way to the fifth floor and was escorted back to a room where I was told to get undressed and get in to one of those nifty backless hospital gowns. I did that. I was laying there minding my own business when Dr. Lyons dropped by the see how I was doing. At that moment I was doing well but the low number on my blood pressure was heading north quickly.

My clothes were in a white bag that the nurse told my wife to leave behind. At that point, it seems, no one was quite sure whether I was going home after the procedure or staying there. Dr. Herbert, by the way, fully intended to have me stay. He told me later there was never a doubt that I was staying.

The rest of it unfolded pretty quickly. At 7:30 I headed downstairs. I was wheeled here and there. At 8 AM it was in to the operating room. People stuck stuff in me. I got a spinal and then some other drug that was supposed to put me in a "twilight" zone. (Rod Serling never showed up) It did, though they tell me we chatted throughout the procedure that took a couple of hours and in which I got 24 needles inserted in me, those needles depositing 78 radioactive seeds each about the size of a grain of rice.

I recall telling them about my baseball card collection, what cards are worth today and how I shot a 76 the week before and beat my cousin Jeff Stevens by one stroke. In a lucid moment that I recalled I told them of three blown putts that could have reduced my

The Glenside Kid

score to a lifetime record 73! Golfers never quit not even sedated ones.

My next hurdle was getting out of the recovery room. They said as soon as (a.) I could feel my feet and make my toes work and (b.) they could find me a bed I'd be out of there. The feet were working for some time when they finally came up with the bed. Since I was radioactive I needed to be in a private room and the guy in mine was taking his time about leaving. Upstairs, I learned later, one nurse had told my wife that I might be in recovery for five hours waiting for that bed. I'm glad they didn't tell me that.

Anyway, I got sprung and got my room and was met by my wife and Nurse Bonnie Klenk who was a real trooper and took very good care of me. My clothes were not there but Bonnie assured me they'd be over by 5:30 PM. At 10 PM that evening my clothes were officially MIA. No one had a clue as to where they were. I had visions of leaving the hospital the next day in my jockey shorts.

Dr. Herbert came in to see me and tell me how well everything had gone and then added that he wouldn't be in the next day. Seems like he was going to play golf. I told him that it was going to 100+ degrees. I wished him well and said up until now I trusted him, but I was beginning to wonder about his judgment. We both laughed.

I was hooked up to all kinds of things, a prisoner in my own bed. And the worst part of that was that I felt just fine. They had an IV in my left hand, had a catheter in (well you know where) and two massage things on my legs that, every minute or two, pumped and pummeled my calves to make sure I didn't get blood clots. I was told that if I need to have a bowel movement it would be bedpan city. I was not happy with that. And as luck would have it I needed the darn thing. Yuck.

Lunch was a spicy roast beef sandwich, dinner a spicy meatloaf. Heartburn was a given. And about 10 PM the heartburn arrived. At Midnight it was quelled by some lemon Maalox.

The Glenside Kid

I didn't sleep much. I never sleep on my back and that was the only option given my marionette-like condition. At intervals throughout the night the nurse came in to take my blood pressure and my temperature. Any sleep that I sandwiched in between visits was a miracle. By 4 AM I was watching the Brett Butler show on TV - it was the best thing on - and later I watched a re-run of the Fox 10 PM News. By 5 AM I was reading a book about facts and myths surrounding Abraham Lincoln's assassination.

Dr. Matt Gerstein was the first to visit me the next morning. He was a resident from Temple and had taken part in my implants. He said I had done fine. Dr. Izes came in soon afterward. I told both doctors about my MIA clothes. Dr. Izes said, "oh great, I can see your column now.'they cured me of cancer but lost my clothes'". It was an idea I was working on. But in no time my personal Florence Nightingale (Nurse Klenk) had come up with clothes and all was getting to be well with the world.

Shortly after that my catheter was removed by an associate of Dr. Herbert's. It was another one of those "take a deep breath" instructions and I was, of course, gasping.

I ate breakfast - two kind of dried out pancakes, one little tub of syrup - and then started gulping water, since I was told I could go home as soon as I urinated. By 9:45 I was ready to go home. It was a great feeling. It was all behind me (no pun intended) and I could truly recite one of my favorite lines.."Today is the first day of the rest of my life".

Once I got over being more tired than usual, I began to feel pretty good again. For the next several weeks I had to wear lead-lined undershorts to protect little kids and pregnant women from any radiation that might be coming from. (I wore the lead-lined pants to Lehigh University on August 15 when I took my 8-year-old Granddaughter Brittany to visit the Eagles practice. When she went home and I took them off I felt 10 pounds lighter.) Most people cannot get any radiation from me - in fact I was told it was questionable if *anyone* could actually be harmed by it. It was explained that the earth probably emits more than I would, but being safe is always a good bet. My wife wondered if I'd glow. Kind of like a night light, but I didn't.

I will be getting regular checkups, they say, for the next five years. That's okay. I stay on top of my health anyway. Would I do anything differently? Absolutely not. I made an informed decision and am confident that, for me, it was the right one.

It was a long seven months and when I look back on it I wonder if there was anything I could or would have done differently. And the answer is no, I feel that I made the right choices based on the information available to me.

Prostate cancer is so common among males it is frightening. But I'm here to tell you that if you are diligent and watchful and catch it in the early stages it is highly curable. Life is a series of episodes. I'm glad and thankful to God, my doctors, my family and friends that there are potentially many more episodes in my lifetime adventure.

The Glenside Kid

Book 2 - The epilogue…

It has now been over eleven years since my treatment. I beat the odds and am doing well. About three years ago the old PSA started north again. This time Dr. Izes attacked it with an implant in my left arm that, he says, I'll get annually as long as I am walking erect. Some call it a chemo drug and it knocks down the PSA – mine is sub 1.0. It also knocks all the stamina out of me for a couple of months. And while I don't like that, it sure beats the alternative. I'm a cancer survivor and I've been a pretty lucky guy my whole life. I'll continue to play the hands that are dealt to me.

As Jean Shepherd said, many times, "Excelsior!"

The Glenside Kid

The author, left, meets his idol Jean Shepherd at Ursinus College in 1970. Note that both writers were fashion-challenged at the time, both wearing plaid pants. Note, also, the dueling sideburns. Perhaps it was the style then. Maybe it was a writer thing.

About the Author

Chestnut Hill College Professor *Henry R. (Ted) Taylor* is a career educator who has been teaching *creative writing* and other related courses at the college since 2000. A career educator, he has been a teacher, baseball coach, administrator and athletics director. In 1989 his Philadelphia College of Textiles & Science baseball team made it to the NCAA Division II Final 8 and while a college AD his teams won a combined 32 championships in various sports.

He is a published author with six books to his credit as well as two college texts. He has been a newspaper columnist and editor, magazine editor and has had countless articles published on a variety of subjects.

He is a lifelong baseball fan, and was the founding president of The Philadelphia Athletics Historical Society that was formed in 1995 to honor the memory of Philadelphia's American League baseball team. His lectures about the A's and their amazing history over 54 years has been delivered in many venues in the tri-state area.

Inspired by Jean Shepherd, and others, Taylor spent many years in radio and TV, a career that paralleled his time in education. He was a disc jockey, play-by-play sportscaster and talk show host on a number of Philadelphia radio stations – including the 50,000 watt WIFI FM regarded by many as one of city's pioneering rock-and-roll outlets. His served as host of a weekly syndicated sports hobby talk show for a number of years and has many numerous TV appearances, including two hosting roles on Fox "In the Zone"

Ted served both Fleer and Score Board as a vice president and headed his own public relations firm. Taylor served as vice chairman of the board of Act II Playhouse, a professional equity theatre (2000-2010) and is a member of the board of the Celestia Performing Arts Association. He has founded several area youth organizations including the Glenside Youth AC, Keystone State Football League and the Warminster Pioneers and was first president of the Eastern Pennsylvania Sports Collectors Club.

The Glenside Kid

Ted is married, the father of four and grandfather of six, and lives with his wife Cindy in Abington, PA and Wildwood Crest NJ.

INDEX

The names listed in the index factor, in some way or other, in to the narrative. Those with incidental mentions, such as a chronology of people living on a particular street, a simple name mention, a group list or a bunch of people attending something or other, probably won't be found here. You will find, however, the names of mostly real people, places and events. In the case of fictionalized characters, whom you will also find, it will be up to you dear reader (if you were from Glenside during the Glenside Kid's days) to figure out who they really are.

My previewers who all tell me that though the story is mostly set in Glenside PA it could have also been Santa Monica CA, Catonsville MD, Kalamazoo MI, Hackensack NJ, Middlebury VT, Greenville SC, Carrollton TX or really any city in America where kids experienced life and its challenges during the middle of the 20th Century. The experience, they say, is a universal one of growing up.

A
Abbott & Costello, 101
Abington Memorial Hospital, 192, 193, 201, 203, 205, 206
Abington Special Police, 146
Abington Township, 43, 44, 146, 155
Acker, Elsie, 143
Aldridge, Kay (Nyoka), 98
American Cancer Society, 199, 200
Andrews, Jack, xviii, xix
Applegate, Helen, 61
Arbuckle, Billy, 57-60
Ashburn, Richie, 104, 138
Atlantic City NJ, 7, 15

Autry, Gene, 24, 51, 72, 98, 99
Avalon NJ, 137, 138

B
Barr, Ron, xviii
Baseball cards, 51, 69, 102-104, 105, 107, 108, 194
Bates, Joe, 32, 105, 137-139
Bath NY, 25
Beaver College (Arcadia University), 7, 71, 159
Beimesderfer, Dr. D. L., 184
Bell, Bert, 40
Bell, Dr. Howard J., 158
Bell, Rev. James, 158, 159
Black Devils Gang, 85-88
Bolaris, John, 90
Brady, Pat, 23, 26
Brissie, Lou, 74
Brooklyn (Los Angeles) Dodgers. 21, 75, 105
Brucker, Earl Sr., 71
Bush, George H. W., 21
Bush, George W., 20, 21
Burnette, Smiley, 98
Buttram, Pat, 98
Buzzard, Charles, 132, 133

C
Cadillac automobiles, 32, 33, 178
Campanella, Roy, 74, 75, 105
Capreri, Eddie, 145
Carmel Presbyterian Church, xv, 52, 55, 155-162, 173
Casa Conti Restaurant, 44, 52
Cassidy, Hopalong, 98
Cats, Siamese, 117, 118
Chapman, Sam, 75
Chamberlain, Wilt, 145
Chatterbox Restaurant (Ocean City, NJ), 14
Chaykosky, Dr. Tim, 109
Cheltenham High School, xiv, xv, xix, 7, 145, 178-181

Cheltenham Township, 43, 146
Chestnut Hill College, xviii, 5, 21, 63
Chevrolet cars, 32, 33
Chicago NFL Cardinals, 37, 39, 41
Chicago Cubs, 76, 77, 103
Chicago White Sox, 71, 75
Chris's Restaurant (Ocean City, NJ), 14
Christ, Jack, 157
Cliff, Albert & Edna, 86
Cliff, Edward, 85-87, 89
Cliff, Karen, 85, 172
Cliff, Richard, 65-67, 85-89, 133
Clyde, Andy, 98
Cookie-the-dog, 119-121, 153
Cors, Al, 50
Crabbe, Buster, 100
Crowder, Buddy, 104, 105

D
Danihel, Charles, 53, 91, 133, 134, 171-177, 181
Danihel, Florence & Joe, 173
Danihel, Jane, 171
Dark, Harry, 130
Dark, Johnny, 128-130
Delaney, Richard, 178
Delanzo, Billy, 132-135
DeLong Hook & Eye Co., 24, 25, 72
Detroit Tigers, 75
Detwiler, Patricia (Lay), 19, 52, 116, 138, 152-154
DiMaggio, Joe, 60
Dobrynin, Helen, 143
Donruss Company, xvii
Doylestown PA, 2, 90
Drexel University, xv, xvi, xix
Duckloe, Norm, 141
Dykes, Jimmy, 71

E

The Glenside Kid

Eby, Dr. James, 161
Eisenhower, Dwight D., 53
Elliott, Wild Bill, 98
Ennis, Del, 103, 104, 138
Evans, Dale, 23
Ewing, Donald Sr., 132-135
Ewing, John, 86, 91, 132, 172

F
Fain, Ferris, 73, 103
Finkeldey, Phil, 22, 143
Finlayson, Harry, 185, 186
Fleer Corporation, xvii, xix, 69, 102
Flynn, Mr., 64, 65
Ford cars, 28, 30-33, 92
Fox Chase Cancer Center, 197, 198
Fox, Nelson, 75
Franks, Tom, 181, 186
Frey, Coach Paul, 143, 144
Friebel, Bill, 178

G
Since the story is basically set in Glenside there are numerous references to the town throughout. To list them all, among other things, would bore you senseless. Assume that Glenside is all over the text.
Gage, Dr. Horace, 110-113
Gage, Dr. George, 110, 111, 113
Gallen, Dr. George, 56
Germany, 7, 9, 29
Gerstein, Dr. Matt, 208
Gifford, Frances (Nyoka), 98
Gillum, Dr. David, 48, 88, 121, 163
Glenside Elementary School, xii, xix, 22, 49, 50, 56-61, 93, 103, 131, 141, 172
Glenside Gorillas football, 53, 174
Glenside Movie theatre, 23, 24
Godfrey, Arthur, ix, 21

Green, Dr. Elaine, 63
Greenberg, Dr. Richard, 198

H
Hager, Jimmy, 86, 91, 133
Hager, Dr. Onslow, 47
Haley, Bill & the Comets, 13
Harmer Hill PA, 7
Harr, David, 22
Harrison, William Welsh, 7, 64
Harting, Dr. Ernest,
Haverford, SS, 4
Hawkins, Walt, 48
Hayden, Russell (Lucky Jenkins), 98
Hayes, Gabby, 23, 98
Haymes, Dick, 100
Haynes, Albert, 86
Helferich, Dr. Donald L., xvi
Heller, Jack, 126, 133
Herbert, Dr. Scott, 201, 204, 206, 207
Hodges, Gil, 105
Hogate's Restaurant (Ocean City, NJ), 14
Holt, Tim, 98
Hudson, Ginny, xiv, 94, 178, 181, 186
Hurlock, David, 133

I
Izes, Dr. Joseph, 203-205, 208, 211

J
Jackson, Reggie, xv
Jenkins, Doris, 12
Jenkins, Madeline (Roth), 7, 19
Jenkintown PA, 24, 32
Johannes, Florence, 22
Johnson, Billy "White Shoes", xvi
Joost, Eddie, 74, 75, 103

The Glenside Kid

K
Katchmer, George, 185
Kennedy, John F., 22
Kellner, Alex, 75
Kerstetter, Sgt. Bob, 146
Kesler, Willis, 157
Keswick Theatre, 23, 24, 100
Kia automobiles, 28
King, Tommy, 85, 87, 132
Kirkland, Donnie, 51, 126
Klenk, Nurse Bonnie, 207, 208
Koch, Bailey & Brittany, 20, 33, 208
Koch, Jeff, 20
Koch, Melissa (Taylor), 20, 151
Konstanty, Jim, 104
Krah, Dr. Edward, 48

L
Lampe, J. Hamilton, 22, 143
Lampe, Dr. John A., 161
Lampkin, Tommy, 49
LaRue, Lash, 98
Lay, Ernie (Uncle/Pop), x, xi, 19, 31, 37, 71-76, 92, 105, 121, 137-140, 152, 179, 181
Lay, Florence (Taylor), 3, 71, 106, 152
Lay, Patricia (see Detwiler)
Leaming, Jim, 69
LeGrande, Coach Mike, 128-131
Leonard, Dutch, 103
Lodge, Mr. & Mrs., 51, 107, 108
Longshore Guest Rooms (Ocean City NJ), 14, 15, 17, 18
Luef, Ralph, 179
LuLu Temple Golf Club (Glenside), 38
Lyons, Dr. Michael, 52, 191, 193, 195-198, 200, 202, 206

M
Mack, Connie, 25, 70-73, 75, 76, 105
Mack, Earle, 71, 75

Magee, Herb, xvii
Majeski, Hank, 73, 74
Manchester, England (UK), 3, 4
Mandler, Dr. John, 194, 196, 197, 206
Martin, Richard (Chito Rafferty), 98
Masters, Janie, 133, 134
Masters, Rich, 133
Mayer, Dr. Donald, 193
Mayer, Dr. Karl, 193
Mays Willie, 105
McAfee, Jane, xiii
McCoskey, Barney, 103
Mercedes Benz, 28, 33
Merklinger, Joe, 105
Miller, Bess (Roth), 7
Millersville State Teacher's College, xi, xv, xix, 32, 179-187
Morin, Dave, 133
Morrison, Bette, 8
Mullan, Paul, xvii
Muller, Elsa, 166
Muller, George (Muller's Flowers), 165, 166, 169
Musial, Stan, 105

N
Nachod, J. Ernest Esq., 108
Neide, Nellie, xiii
Newcombe, Don, 105
Niagara Falls NY, 8, 25, 27
Niagara, Joe (WIBG Radio), 21
Nyoka, Queen of the Jungle, 98, 99, 101

O
Ocean City NJ, 13-19, 32, 180
Oliver, Chippy, 126, 133-135
O'Brien, Larry (Glenn Miller Orchestra), 24
O'Malley, Dillon "Snavely", 82-84, 86, 90, 91, 126, 133
O'Malley, Dr. Sean "Pig", 83
O'Malley, Peter, 21

Ontario Canada, 24, 25, 27
Our Lady Help of Christians RC Church, 155
Oxford University (England), xvi

P
Parks, Henry, 61
Patton, Cliff, 42
Pennsylvania, University of, 35, 181
Peterson, Joe, 94, 95
Philadelphia Athletics, ix, 35, 60, 70-76, 105, 128, 213
Philadelphia Bulletin, 52, 163, 164
Philadelphia College of Textiles & Science, xviii, xix
Philadelphia Daily News, 102
Philadelphia Eagles, 37-42, 208
Philadelphia Inquirer, 104
Philadelphia Phillies, ix, x, 35, 75-77. 104-106, 138
Philadelphia PGA, xvii
Plymouth cars, 25, 28-31, 107
Pontiac cars, 28
Prostate Cancer, 191, 193-195, 209

R
Reading Railroad (Glenside Station), 39, 110, 167
Reagan, Ronald, 20
Red Rascal Roller Skates, 115, 116
Reeves, George, 100
Refsnyder, Dick, 48, 126, 132-134
Reigel, Skee, 49
Renninger, Carol, 48, 122, 123
Renninger, Gladys & Kendall, 122, 123
Renninger, Harry, 53, 54
Repinski, Matt, 105, 137
Richter, Dr. Melvin, 197, 198, 200, 206
Riley, Gene, 80
Roatche, Charlotte, 22
Roberts, Robin, 104, 105
Robinson, Bill, 48, 175
Robinson, Fred, 178

Robinson, Jackie, 105
Ronnie's 5&10 (Glenside), 51, 80, 104, 106-108
Rogers, Roy, 23, 24, 26. 57, 58, 65, 72, 98
Roosevelt, Franklin D., ix, 21
Roosevelt, Theodore "Teddy", 56, 67
Rosen, Steve & Marty, 48
Rosenfeld Cancer Center (Abington Hospital), 201, 203
Roth, Bess (Miller), 7
Roth, Clara (see Sines)
Roth, Dick, 67
Roth, George, 10, 11
Roth, Harry, 7, 10, 11
Roth, Helen (Mom, Taylor, Lay), x, xi, 7, 8, 17, 18, 25, 29, 31, 38, 50, 78-81, 88, 107, 108, 110, 113, 116, 120-122, 137, 138, 140, 144, 152, 153, 157, 164, 167, 181
Roth, Henry, 9
Roth, Irma (Kaltenegger), 9, 10, 79, 81
Roth, Karl & Katarina, 7
Roth, Lena (Kohl), 10
Roth, Madeline (Jenkins), 7
Roth, Phillip E., 7, 9, 10
Roth, Rudy, 10, 11, 79
Rum & Coke (A person, not the drink), 65
Ruestle, Elsie & Jim, 180
Ruestle, Rusty, 179, 180

S
Samuel, Mayor Bernard, 73
Sauer, Hank, 76, 77
Scott, Carolyn, xiii, 122, 133, 134
Scranton PA, 25
Seminick, Andy, 104
Shepherd, Florence, xii
Shepherd, Jean, 1, 22, 58, 171, 211-213
Shibe Park (Philadelphia), 36, 71, 82, 128
Simmons, Al, 71, 74
Simmons, Curt, 77, 138
Sines, Barbara, 29, 30

Sines, Buddy, 29, 37
Sines, Charles, 29, 37-40, 42, 47, 119, 120, 123
Sines, Clara (Roth), 10, 29, 37, 38, 47, 119, 123
Sisler, Dick, 105
Sizemore, Eleanor, 179
Slade, Captain Bill, 147
Slater, Patrick, 133
Snider, Duke, 105
Snyder, Billy, 15
Snyder, Grandma, 15, 17, 18
Snyder, Peggy, 15
Sons of the Pioneers, 23, 25-37
Spencer, Nick, 133
Spring Garden College, xvi, 5, 102
Stabely, George, 22
Stauffer, Miss, 142
Stevens, Jeff, 206
St. John, Fuzzy, 98
St. Martin's-in-the-Fields Church (Chestnut Hill), 5
Steele, Bob, 98
Steel Pier (Atlantic City NJ), 15
Sticker, Merritt, 32, 94
Strand Hotel (Ocean City, NJ), 17, 18
Strange, Larry, 60, 142, 143
Stremic, Jerry, 142, 143
Sudlow, Dorothy, xiii

T
(Since this book is about Ted Taylor's life and he's mentioned throughout it, it won't be hard to locate him in here. But in the interest of space – and saving a tree or two – no actual page listings will be included for him.)
Taggart, Esther, 49, 56, 58
Tate, Mayor James H. J., 74
Taylor Business School, 7
Taylor, Brett & Colleen, 1, 12, 33, 34, 43, 78, 90, 96, 109, 117, 124, 136, 151, 170

Taylor, Brett II & Lily, 1, 34, 35, 43, 63, 69, 96, 109, 117, 124, 136, 151
Taylor, Chris & Lisa, 28, 136
Taylor, Cynthia (DeMarco), xiv, xvi, 1, 14, 33-35, 63, 69, 82, 83, 90, 114, 171, 194, 197, 209
Taylor, Henry (Jack/Dad), ix, x, xi, 3, 5, 6, 8, 13, 16-18, 24-27, 29, 37, 49, 72, 78, 79
Taylor, John, 2-5, 8, 12
Taylor, John Henry, 3
Taylor, John Joseph, 3
Taylor, June, 179
Taylor, Mary Ann (Hill), 3, 12, 13, 71
Taylor, Mary Sarah, 3
Temple University, xiii, 35, 44, 141
Thomas, Barbara, 179
Thomas Williams Junior High (Wyncote PA), xiii, xix, 141-144, 172
Thompson, Tommy, 42
Thornton, Dr. James, 161
Truman, Harry S, 21, 22
Tully, John, xv, xvi

U-V
Ulmer, Claude Rothermel, 186
United States, SS, 11
Ursinus College, xvi, 124
Van Buren, Steve, 41
Verban, Emil "The Antelope", 103
Vienna (Austria), 9, 10

W
Walters, Bucky & Carolyn, 142
Wambold, Bobby, 128, 130, 133, 165, 167
Waughtel, Evelyn, 59
Waxman, Lew, 51
Weaver, John, 142
Weirich, Coach Hal, 185-187
Westerman, Bob, 104

Whipple, Joe, 104, 105, 126
White Pharmacy (Glenside), 103
Widener College (PMC), xvi
Wiedler, Joe, 133
Wildwood, NJ, 6, 12, 13, 214
Willow Grove Park PA, 44, 147-150
Wilson, Walter "Dipper", xiii, xiv, 47
Worthington, Al, 167-169
Worthington, Dr. Edward, 142
Wyrostek, Johnny, 142

Y
YMCA (Abington), 173, 174
Yugo car, 33

Z
Zeigenfuss, Dot, 157
Zimmerman, Shorty, 50
Zorro, 100, 101

Special thanks

To: My wife Cynthia M. Taylor who supports me in all these endeavors, my lifelong friend Chuck Danihel who plugged in some missing spaces, my publisher Bob Sims who is a dream to work with, my PR guru Leza Raffel (Communications Solutions Group), my friends and colleagues at Chestnut Hill College who keep encouraging me to "write more" – Dr. Elaine Green, Dr. Ken Soprano, Walter Childs, Donna Smith, Marie Scheetz, Christine Nydick; my children (and their spouses) – Brett & Colleen Taylor, Chris & Lisa Taylor and Jeff & Melissa Taylor Koch; my dear friends Nan and Jack Andrews, Emerson and Sharon Shaw, Gene and Diana Bonetti, Jeff and Charlotte Stevens and Dr. Michael Lyons who all inspire me to greater heights. And to all of you who have read this far. Thank you.

Acknowledgement

All authors/writers are inspired by the works of others. I am no different. Jean Shepherd was one of my earliest inspirations (the man could flat out tell a story), but I also love the works and style of Robert B. Parker (the King of dialogue and short chapters), Max Allen Collins (who takes history and uses it to tell a story in a way few others can), Jack Higgins (a master mystery writer), Elliott Roosevelt (who made his mother, Eleanor, a great detective) and Margaret Truman (who knew how to craft characters and weave them in to multiple story lines). Lately the works of Laura Hillenbrand (Sea Biscuit and Unbroken) have captivated me. There are other authors

The Glenside Kid

whose works I enjoy, but the aforementioned could rewrite the phone book and make it a compelling read.